Stonewall Jackson

and

Winchester, Virginia

Stonewall Jackson

and Winchester, Virginia

Jerry Holsworth

The History Press

Published by The History Press
Charleston, SC 29403
www.historypress.net

First published 2012

Manufactured in the United States

ISBN 978.1.60949.530.5

Library of Congress CIP data applied for.

This book is dedicated to the memory of

Mrs. Mabel Aikin

Contents

Preface

A year ago, my friend and fellow historian Ben Ritter suggested that I write a magazine article on Stonewall Jackson and Winchester, Virginia. After the wonderful job that The History Press did with my first book, *Civil War Winchester*, I suggested that it would be a better idea to contact the publisher and see if it was interested. The result is this book. Before I begin to thank everyone who helped make this book possible, I must begin by saying that this book is equally the work of Ben Ritter.

For over a half century, Ben has researched Winchester's part in the American Civil War, with an emphasis on the Stonewall Brigade. For this book, he kindly gave me access to all of that material. What I found was a treasure-trove of information, much of it never before seen in either books or magazine articles. In fact, there was too much information for the limited space of this book. The reality is that I wrote this book, but the massive amount of research that was necessary was entirely the work of Ben Ritter, and it is equally his creation.

The study of the life of Stonewall Jackson is perhaps one of the most exhaustive of any of the great leaders of the Civil War. Over the past century and a half, many books, several of them massive in content, and innumerable magazine and newspaper articles have been written about the general. What Ben was driving at, and what I have tried to write, is not intended to be a comprehensive study of Jackson.

This book focuses on two major themes: what Winchester, Virginia, thought about Stonewall Jackson, and what he thought about the Valley town. There may be parts of this book with which the devoted student of

Jackson might disagree. There are countless stories about Jackson and his many peculiarities. Some of them are ridiculous, like the legend that Jackson was as obsessed with sucking lemons as a chain smoker is with cigarettes.

Another is that Jackson slept through almost every church service he attended. Although many good historians believe this, the rumor is roundly disputed in this book. It is challenged not because I strongly disagree with the premise but because Winchester deeply resented it. It is nearly impossible to prove who is correct, but it is quite easy to prove what the people of Winchester and, in particular, Jackson's pastor, Dr. James R. Graham, thought. He and several other Winchester citizens wrote passionately about this story on several occasions.

In addition to Ben Ritter, I would also like to acknowledge the work of several authors who have paved the way for any study of Stonewall Jackson and Winchester, Virginia. No one who wishes to write about Stonewall Jackson can do so successfully without consulting these great books. The best biography of Stonewall Jackson is *Stonewall Jackson: The Man, the Soldier, the Legend* by Dr. James I. Robertson. It is not only comprehensive in its coverage of the general, but it is also balanced and free of some of the more fantastic legends that surround Jackson.

There are four other books on Winchester during the Civil War that were invaluable. Margaretta Barton Colt's *Defend the Valley* is still my favorite and, in my opinion, one of the best Civil War books ever written. *Beleaguered Winchester* by Dr. Richard Duncan and *Winchester in the Civil War* by Roger Delauter are both invaluable sources for information on the Valley town's Civil War experience. Garland Quarles's book, *Occupied Winchester*, although written many years ago, is still one of the best of its kind. Any writer who wishes to cover any aspect of Winchester during the Civil War era must begin and end with these four wonderful books. For information on the regiments of the Stonewall Brigade and the soldiers from Winchester who fought in that storied brigade, H.E. Howard's Virginia Regimental Series proved to be a very helpful resource.

Of course, no book on Winchester is possible without the almost inexhaustible resources found at the Stewart Bell Jr. Archives, Handley Regional Library, in Winchester. Rebecca Ebert and the rest of the staff were a great help in putting together this book and its illustrations, and I would like to thank them for their help. Cissy Shull and Sherry Jenkins were also very helpful in providing materials for this book, particularly concerning the history of Stonewall Jackson's Headquarters, and the *Winchester–Frederick County Historical Society Journal* is one of best resources available for any era of Winchester history.

Preface

For a book like this one, illustrations are always a critical element in its success. Old photographs are difficult to find, and in many cases, it's equally difficult to bring out the quality necessary for publication. Tina Helms at the historical society is a master at making these photographs work, and I would like to thank her for the wonderful job she did. Finding good illustrations always requires tapping into a number of sources, and I would like to thank all of them for the use of their materials. Several of the credits are labeled with abbreviations. The ones from the Ben Ritter/Garland Quarles Collection are labeled BR/GQ, those from the Winchester–Frederick County Historical Society are WFCHS and those from the Stewart Bell Jr. Archives, Handley Regional Library, are THL.

The maps used in this book were provided by Wilbur Johnston, the very best mapmaker of Frederick County and Winchester since Jedediah Hotchkiss roamed the Shenandoah Valley. His maps are available for purchase through the Winchester–Frederick County Historical Society and are well worth the price.

Michael A. Lynn of the Stonewall Jackson Foundation provided the photographs of Mrs. Jackson after the war with her child and great-granddaughter, as well as the color photograph of Stonewall Jackson's home in Lexington, Virginia. I would also like to thank the people at Stonewall Jackson's House in Lexington for their uniform kindness and cooperation on this project. Diane Jacob, archivist at the Preston Library, Virginia Military Institute, was also a great help, providing several excellent pictures of Mary Anna Jackson. Debbie Butler and Donna Saville of the Shenandoah Apple Blossom Festival were generous enough to provide me with rare pictures of Katherine Creech and Mary Tyler Moore. The National Archives provided the pictures of several characters in this book, as well as a picture of Harpers Ferry from the Civil War. Most of the pictures and illustrations come from the Stewart Bell Jr. Archives, Handley Regional Library, and the private collection of the late Garland Quarles. To all of you, my many thanks.

Besides written sources and illustrations, help came from several individuals who provided me with their expertise on particular subjects. Di Cornell, who for many years has been researching the Shenandoah Apple Blossom queens, was able to provide me with a treasure-trove of data on Katherine Creech. Di also helped me get in contact with Mrs. Cortlandt Freeman, the great-granddaughter of Stonewall Jackson and the older sister of Ms. Creech. Mrs. Freeman's interview and Di's research were indispensible.

Kernstown Battlefield Association president Gary Crawford and Handley boys' cross country coach Mark Stickley both sat down with me for long interviews, and it is through their kindness that the story of the Kernstown Battlefield Association is part of this book. Last but not least, I would like to thank my proofreader, Helene Becker, for her usual outstanding job of correcting my many errors.

Introduction

May 31, 1862, was a day to remember for the troops of Major General Thomas J. "Stonewall" Jackson's small army. Having completed a dazzling offensive movement that was the cornerstone of one of the most brilliant military campaigns in American history, the army had just escaped a trap that might have turned the campaign's achievements into disaster.

Beginning on April 30, Jackson's army had marched over 150 miles in thirty days from its camp near Swift Run Gap to the banks of the Potomac River. During that period, it had fought four successful battles and routed two Union armies. The maneuver had sent shockwaves through the Federal government in Washington, D.C., and lifted the spirits of the new Confederate States of America to new heights after the new country suffered through one of its lowest points during the war.

The Federal government, however, was in no mood to let Jackson's army rest on its laurels and sent two Union forces immediately to the Shenandoah Valley to trap them near the town of Strasburg, Virginia. Through a series of marches through rain and humid weather, most of Jackson's army had escaped the trap and was now relatively safe in its encampments near Strasburg. Only the Stonewall Brigade was not there, but after enduring a grueling two-day march from Harpers Ferry, it had safely arrived at Newtown, just ten miles north of Strasburg.

Taking advantage of a well-deserved rest, Captain Campbell Brown, a member of Major General Richard Ewell's staff, whose division was part of Jackson's command, took time to pen a letter to his mother. He wrote, "Our old chief Jackson is the very man to be put in the Valley of Virginia, for he believes altogether in its importance & it would be hard to convince him that the axis of the world does not stick somewhere between Winchester and Lexington."

It is doubtful that Brown understood the depth of the accuracy of his words. The young staff officer had only known Jackson for less than a month and could not have known that his phrase "axis of the world does not stick somewhere between Winchester and Lexington" described, in near perfect detail, the thought processes and emotional grounding for Jackson's amazing campaign. Deep within Jackson was a love for the Shenandoah Valley in general, and the towns of Lexington and Winchester in particular, that had driven him from the first moments of the war.

Stonewall Jackson is one of the most enigmatic figures of the Civil War. His personality and emotional makeup have been the subjects of countless biographies, books and magazine articles that stretch over a period of 150 years. The complexity of his personality is impossible to cover within the pages of this small book. Needless to say, many historians over the last 150 years have attempted, and failed, to capture the essence of the man Stonewall Jackson.

It is not surprising that Jackson is such a difficult person to know. He was a deeply shy man and rarely let his emotions get control of him. Because of his fame and personality, eyewitness accounts have seemed to exaggerate many of his habits, resulting in a distorted view of the man. Many see Jackson as a general riding on a tiny horse with one arm raised in prayer, the other pumping up and down to help relieve some imagined ailment, with a lemon stuck in his mouth. Such caricatures only deepen the misunderstandings.

Jackson was many things, and many of them, at first glance, seem contradictory. To sort out all of that is not the intention of this book. Here, the emphasis will not be on Jackson's personality but rather his relationship with the Shenandoah Valley and one town in particular: Winchester, Virginia. Subjects such as his health issues and how he dealt with them, his generalship, his Christian faith and his yearning for a home and family will be dealt with only in relationship to how they affected Winchester and its people. The primary time frame for the book begins with Jackson's assignment to command at Harpers Ferry and will carry through the end of the 1862 Valley Campaign.

It was during this period that Jackson and the citizens of Winchester got to know each other, and their relationship blossomed. During his stay in and around Winchester between November 1861 and his departure in early March 1862, both Jackson and his wife forged intimate relationships with the townspeople that lasted long after the general's untimely death following the Battle of Chancellorsville. Almost everyone in Winchester had strong opinions about Jackson and expressed them freely over a long period of time. For several decades after Jackson's death, the local newspaper, the *Evening Star*, ran regular columns about Jackson and the citizens of Winchester. Many of these accounts stretch credulity but are nonetheless revealing in their judgment of Jackson and his place in the history of their community.

As the war progressed, the town began to understand that its role in the war was to be that of a battlefield, and this certainly tempered its opinion of the generals involved in the struggle for the town. For those who embraced the Southern cause, Jackson represented their protector. Mrs. Mary Greenhow Lee, the most prolific of several Winchester diarists, told Jackson in the fall of 1862, "On you and you alone we depend."

Jackson and his wife's opinions of Winchester were equally strong. His answer to Mrs. Lee was that if it were his choice, "Winchester would be his headquarters." Jackson stated early in the war that he believed "If the Valley is lost, Virginia is lost." That phrase could be interpreted in many ways, including an emotional one. Jackson certainly saw the Shenandoah Valley and western Virginia as home, and in many ways, it was from that perspective that he fought for its safety. This was a feeling that was shared by the citizens of Winchester, as well as the rest of the Valley. The assertion could easily be restated by the citizens of Winchester: "If Jackson is lost, the Valley is lost." The magnitude of the grief expressed by the town following his death is a clear testament to that belief.

The story of Jackson's love for the Shenandoah Valley begins with his resignation from the United States Army and the start of his career as a professor at the Virginia Military Institute in Lexington, Virginia, in 1851. The larger community Jackson entered in 1852 was truly unique. Settled over one hundred years after the Tidewater Region in eastern Virginia, the Shenandoah Valley had little in common with its neighbors on the eastern side of the Blue Ridge Mountains. The first settlers to the Shenandoah Valley were German and Scots-Irish; they traveled from the port at Philadelphia south and west along the Great Wagon Road, later known as the Valley Turnpike.

Arriving in the Valley for the first time in the 1730s, these immigrants were of the Lutheran and Presbyterian faiths, as well as English Quakers. Known collectively as "dissenters," they had traveled to the New World to escape religious persecution in their homelands. Intensely religious, they wanted no part of a government-sponsored, established religion. This widened the gap between the non-English setters in the Valley and their Anglican counterparts to the east. Severe persecution from the established Anglican Church was not an uncommon occurrence, and bad feelings ran high between these two Virginias—and not just for religious reasons.

The religious denominations in the Valley had little use for the lifestyle of the planter class in the rest of Virginia, and that was particularly true when it came to the institution of slavery. Most farmers in the Valley did not use slaves and chose to work their land themselves. When they did use African Americans, it was, for the most part, as employees. Most citizens of the Valley were indifferent to slavery, but some, particularly among the Quakers, were openly hostile to it and were likely active in the Underground Railroad movement.

It was in this environment that Jackson began his duties as a professor at the Virginia Military Institute (VMI). Having been an avid student of the Bible and Christianity from an early age, the new professor almost immediately set out to find a church home in Lexington. Studying carefully each of the denominations in town, he settled on the Presbyterian Church, and from that point forward his Christian faith grew rapidly. Many of his contemporaries, as well as later historians, believed that Jackson's newfound faith turned him into a fanatic and saw his particular way of practicing his Christian faith as a source of derision and peculiarity.

That was not true of his neighbors in the Shenandoah Valley who saw Jackson's method of practicing Christianity as, for the most part, nothing unusual. After the war, his pastor and closest friend in Winchester, James Graham, wrote a long essay defending Jackson's faith. Graham saw nothing unusual or odd about Jackson. This was an opinion that was shared by a great many of the people of Winchester and the Shenandoah Valley. It was, after all, through them that he developed his system of practicing Christianity.

During his time in Lexington, Jackson refined his social graces and became part of the town's economic life. He also married Elinor Junkin, the daughter of the president of Washington College, not only bringing him a wife but attaching him socially to a locally prominent family as well. Moving in with the Junkin family, Jackson's domestic happiness was not destined to last long. Soon after their marriage, Elinor became pregnant, and the thought of becoming a father brought Jackson overwhelming joy. When both the child and Elinor died during childbirth, Jackson was devastated.

He had dealt with tragedy all his life, but this blow was almost more than he could bear. His Christian faith had grown so strong that it aided him immensely in dealing with the tragedy. Describing Jackson's coping mechanisms, Presbyterian minister Dr. Moses D. Hoge recalled, "Leaving out the religious element, would be like undertaking to describe Switzerland without mentioning the Alps."

It was only a matter of time, though, before the giant hole in Jackson's life caused by Elinor's death needed to be filled, and he again turned to the daughter of a Presbyterian minister. Jackson married Mary Anna Morrison, the daughter of Dr. Robert H. Morrison, founding president of Davidson College in North Carolina. For the next three years, the couple enjoyed a blissful life together, but not without tragedy. The couple lost their first child shortly after its birth.

By the time war arrived in April 1861, Jackson was firmly established in Lexington, both professionally and socially. His position on the war was firmly on the side of states' rights, and he completely embraced the Southern cause when Virginia seceded. On April 21, 1861, Jackson marched the VMI cadets out of Lexington for Richmond, where they were needed to drill and train the new recruits who were pouring into the new Confederate capital from all over the South.

About one hundred miles to the north, the citizens of Winchester were also preparing for the inevitable. Militia companies with names like the Continental Morgan Guard, Winchester Rifles and Marion Rifles were assembling and marching north to Harpers Ferry, the rallying point for troops from the Shenandoah Valley. Many other young men in Winchester were heading for Harpers Ferry unattached to any militia company. Some traveled in a group they proudly dubbed the "Boomerangs."

Most had never heard of the professor from VMI who would eventually lead them in some of the most stirring campaigns in military history. One who had was Charles Marshall Barton, who had been a student of Jackson at VMI and had written a poem about him while a cadet. As he stepped off his front porch onto Cameron Street to travel to Harpers Ferry, little did he realize that just over a year later he would die within a mile and a half of that front porch as part of a dramatic quest with his former professor to retake his hometown.

He was not alone. These young men of Winchester rushing from their homes were, along with the rest of the town's citizens, forming a historic bond with the professor that still lives to this day.

1

"Me Thinks I See the Stamp of Genius on His Brow"

It was decided, but only after a heated and lengthy debate. The delegates to the Virginia Secession Convention had been divided, their positions on the issue mostly determined by region, and almost all the delegates west of the Blue Ridge Mountains were adamantly opposed to it. Unlike their "to the manor born" neighbors to the east, Virginians from west of the Blue Ridge were yeoman farmers, shopkeepers and mechanics who had no interest in leaving the Union over slavery or states' rights. Led by Robert Y. Conrad of Winchester, Virginia, the westerners had managed to keep the Old Dominion in the Union thus far.

Despite the initial success, Conrad was frustrated that the states in the lower South and the Federal government seemed strangely united to bring about civil war. South Carolina had fired on Fort Sumter on April 12, 1861, and President Abraham Lincoln, who had refused to see a delegation from Virginia sent to Washington expressly to avoid war, had responded by calling for troops to put down the rebellion. Virginia was called on to raise two regiments to join Lincoln's invasion of the Southern states. This latest action by the new president removed all contentiousness from the convention, and the state promptly seceded.

With the need to quickly build a defense force against this threat, Governor John Letcher called for volunteers. Enthusiasm was high, and the governor had little trouble raising recruits, but who would train them? The solution, Letcher felt, was back in his hometown of Lexington, Virginia, where 176 cadets at the Virginia Military Institute were well trained in the art of war. Their commandant, Major Thomas J. Jackson, must bring them to Richmond at once.

Near dawn on Sunday, April 21, Jackson received the order to bring the cadets to Richmond. Acting quickly, he had his charges marching north toward the railroad in Staunton, Virginia, at exactly 12:30 p.m. that afternoon. They were picked up a few miles from town by the Harman Brothers stagecoach line and taken to Staunton, where they boarded trains for Richmond. Once the cadets were assigned to the different companies, though, their commandant had little to do.

Having served with distinction in the artillery during the Mexican War and trained the VMI cadets in that arm for almost ten years at the institute, Jackson kept busy visiting and advising the different batteries assembled outside Richmond while he waited for an assignment. When those orders arrived, he was shocked and disappointed, but with his cadets all around him he was required to set a proper example. Orders were to be obeyed, not questioned.

Jackson was ordered to report to the topographical engineers with the rank of major. Not only was the assignment ignoring his military experience as an artillerist, but also drawing was his worse course at West Point! He made no public complaint, but his wife, Mary Anna Jackson, recalled later, "It was distasteful to him, because he felt that he could not render as much service in it as by more active service in the field." Fortunately for Jackson and the Confederacy, friends in Richmond were equally outraged and immediately took steps to have him transferred. Jonathan M. Bennett, a lawyer from Jackson's boyhood home, Weston, Virginia, was in Richmond. In 1842, a much younger Jackson had arrived at Bennett's office with a request for a letter of introduction to Congressman Samuel L. Hays. Jackson was seeking an appointment to the United States Military Academy. Bennett had reservations since the youth seemed severely handicapped academically, but Jackson's determination came through during his interview, and Bennett wrote the letter.

Nearly twenty years later, Jackson's achievements in both the army and at VMI proved that Bennett's decision to write that introduction was a wise one. The Weston lawyer immediately sought out Virginia governor John Letcher and strongly suggested that Jackson be assigned to field command. Letcher, a neighbor of Jackson in Lexington, was in complete agreement. On April 26, the Virginia governor promoted Jackson to colonel and the next day called him into his office and assigned him command at Harpers Ferry.

Overjoyed to be relieved of his duties as an engineer, Jackson left immediately for his new post. Traveling by rail, he reached Strasburg in the Shenandoah Valley and arrived in Winchester about midday on April 28. There he attended to a few military matters and wrote a short letter to his

Stonewall Jackson's Home in Lexington, Virginia. *Courtesy of the Stonewall Jackson Foundation, Lexington, Virginia.*

wife, Mary Anna, stating, "I am very much gratified with my command, and would rather have this post than any other in the state." It was doubtful that anyone took much notice of Jackson's arrival in Winchester. His stay was short, and he was on his way to Harpers Ferry via the Winchester and Potomac Railroad within hours after his arrival there.

Jackson's new post was one of the most beautiful spots in Virginia. Thomas Jefferson had described the scenery there as worth a trip across the Atlantic Ocean. Although Jackson always appreciated such beauty, it was hardly on his mind as he arrived at his new command. Harpers Ferry was one of the most strategic sites in Virginia, and defending it and training the troops there were his top priorities.

Located at the confluence of the Potomac and Shenandoah Rivers, the Baltimore and Ohio (B&O) Railroad crossed the Potomac there, and the Chesapeake and Ohio (C&O) Canal passed by just across the Potomac from the town. Both were vital supply links for coal and wheat for Washington, D.C., and other East Coast cities. A major arms manufacturing center, which had been the target of John Brown's Raid in 1859, was located there as well. Unfortunately, Harpers Ferry was also dominated on all sides by heights that made it almost impossible to defend.

Civil War Harpers Ferry. *Courtesy of the National Archives.*

The post was home to at least two thousand new recruits, all commanded by an assortment of militia officers, most of whom were high on show and low on experience. There was no real organizational level at Harpers Ferry higher than a company, and the post was dangerously short on equipment, weapons, ammunition and other military essentials. Recruits lived in homes, warehouses or any other place available, and there was no hospital. What Jackson inherited was a menagerie of militia officers and their staffs, which gave the place more the air of a pageant than that of a military base.

Jackson's task was eased somewhat by an order issued by Governor Letcher just before his arrival relieving all militia officers above the rank of captain. Most left for home in disgust after their demotion, leaving the new commander open to appoint whomever he pleased to replace them. Another welcome sight was several VMI cadets who were there as drill instructors, as well as several graduates of the institute scattered among the soldiers.

To begin organizing this loose collection of recruits required a professional staff, and Jackson immediately began to assemble one. His first appointments were individuals he knew well. The position of assistant adjutant general went to Major John Thomas Lewis Preston, who acted as Jackson's chief of staff. Preston was one of the co-founders of VMI and had recently married

Margaret Junkin, the sister of Jackson's first wife, Elinor. Major James W. Massie, an instructor at VMI, was assigned to the position of inspector general.

Another interesting appointment was Major John A. Harman as quartermaster. Harman was a partner in the stagecoach company of Harman and Brothers and was responsible for transporting Jackson and the VMI cadets from Lexington to Staunton for both the execution of John Brown in 1859 and their trip to Richmond a month earlier. Short tempered and accustomed to outbursts of foul language, Harman was unlike any other staff officer who served under Jackson during the entire war.

While at Harpers Ferry, Harman also played a part in providing Jackson with his most famous mount, Little Sorrell. After Harman captured several boxcars filled with cattle and horses on the Baltimore and Ohio Railroad, Jackson came by to inspect the captured animals. Seeing two Sorrel horses that he liked and having no mount of his own at the time, he purchased them from the Confederate government, which, according to Jackson's strict view of things, owned all the captured animals.

Intending to use the larger horse for his mount, Jackson planned to send the smaller one to his wife. But when the larger animal proved too unmanageable, he tried the smaller one. Jackson became so fond of the horse that he kept it for himself. Little Sorrell became his favorite mount, and he rode her throughout all his subsequent campaigns; he was even riding her when he received his fatal wound at Chancellorsville.

Another of Jackson's new staff members was an unofficial one. Winchester native Francis B. Jones was appointed to the position of assistant adjutant general on May 10. Known as Frank to his friends, Jones possessed one of the finest Shenandoah Valley pedigrees of anyone at Harpers Ferry. The great-grandson of Gabriel Jones, Thomas Lord Fairfax's lawyer, Jones had just missed having Jackson as a professor, graduating from VMI in 1848. Now in his early thirties, Jones was married with two small children and was farming just south of Winchester.

It is doubtful that Jackson knew Jones personally, although they might have met at VMI before the war. The two, however, certainly had at least one important mutual acquaintance. As a boy, Jones had attended the Episcopal School in Alexandria, Virginia, whose principal at the time was William N. Pendleton. Pendleton later served as the rector of the Episcopal church in Lexington. He was at Harpers Ferry as the commander of the Rockbridge Artillery, and his son Sandie had been appointed to Jackson's staff as an aide. Pendleton could have given Jones a recommendation, and being an alum of VMI was probably a factor, too.

Jackson must have placed great value on the role Jones was playing at his headquarters. During the war, Jackson developed a reputation of rewarding efficiency with more work, and Jones seemed to have more than he could handle. Jones wrote to his wife on April 23, "This is the first spare moment that I have had since I've been here, and I have no time to go into detail." He added, "I hold an office whose duties are new to me & being ignorant & exceedingly engaged by orders and inquires from every body I am greatly engaged."

Although overburdened, Jones was pragmatic enough to appreciate the advantages he had. Several close family members who were at Harpers Ferry were not faring nearly as well as he:

> *I cannot believe it possible that I will be retained in so important an office. I assure you that life in the line is horrid, do not say so before sister F or Mrs. Barton but I assure you that of a private in the ranks is desperate, they have by no means the shelter of my own cattle, there are hundreds of men out, exposed to all kinds of weather with nothing but a blanket, night & day.*

Dr. Hunter McGuire, who looked so young in this first interview that Jackson checked with Richmond to see if there had been some mistake before appointing him medical director of the Stonewall Brigade. *Courtesy of BR/GQ.*

Jones was surprised and pleased to report, though, "I am certain that I have given complete satisfaction so far to the Col., he has without my suggesting it written twice to the Governor urging my (permanent) appointment."

Later that month, he wrote to his mother about his new commander, describing him as "a member of the Presbyterian church, one of the most conscientious men I know, pious, determined and brave. I like him very much, very fair very polite, he has very little to say, but I have a vast deal of confidence in him."

Jones was not the only Winchester resident to be assigned to Jackson's staff, and the second one shocked Jackson. A young private in the Winchester Rifles, who also happened to be a doctor, was reassigned by Richmond to Jackson's staff. Private Hunter McGuire, a tall, thin twenty-six-year-old, looked ten years younger than his true age. Upon arriving at Jackson's headquarters to report for duty, McGuire stated:

> *He looked at me for a long time without saying a word, and presently said, "You can go back to your quarters and wait there until you hear from me." I went back to my quarters and didn't hear from him for a week, when one evening I was announced at dress parade as medical director of the army. Some months afterwards, when I asked the General the cause of the delay, he said that I looked so young that he had sent to Richmond to see if there wasn't some mistake.*

Jackson would soon learn of his good luck with the assignment of McGuire to his military family. The son of Dr. Hugh McGuire, Hunter, like his father, was something of a prodigy. His father, at the same age, had founded the Winchester Medical College, the first medical school in Virginia. After working with his father as a boy and actually completing several courses as a teenager, Hunter attended the prestigious Jefferson Medical College in Philadelphia, Pennsylvania. At twenty-two, he returned to Winchester and took a position on the faculty at his father's medical school. Like many of his friends, when war broke out in April 1861, McGuire enlisted as a private in the Winchester Rifles and was practicing his new trade of infantryman at Harpers Ferry when it was discovered that his skills were being underutilized.

Jackson quickly and efficiently made progress with the raw recruits until he was replaced by General Joseph E. Johnston on May 23, 1861. Johnston assigned Jackson to the command of all the Virginia forces at the post. Organized into a brigade made up entirely of soldiers from the Shenandoah Valley, it comprised the Second, Fourth, Fifth and the Twenty-seventh Virginia Infantries, as well as the Rockbridge Artillery.

Confederate soldiers preparing to leave for Harpers Ferry in 1861 from the Market House at the corner of Boscawen and Cameron Streets in downtown Winchester. Notice the tracks of the Winchester and Potomac Railroad in the center of Cameron Street. *Courtesy of BR/GQ.*

Jackson's new brigade was truly a family affair. All the companies among the five units were recruited by county and made up of family members and old acquaintances, many of whom had close prewar ties to Jackson. Commanding the Second Virginia Infantry was Colonel James Allen, a classmate of Frank Jones at VMI and a mathematics professor with Jackson at the institute before the war. One of the company commanders in the regiment, Lawson Botts, was also a classmate of Jones and Allen at VMI. Botts, a Jefferson County native, gained some notoriety before the war while serving briefly as John Brown's defense attorney. A private in Company B was Shepherdstown native Alexander Boteler Jr., the son of an important political figure in the Valley and a warm personal friend and advocate of Jackson. The company commander of the Winchester Rifles was William L. Clark Jr., the brother of Jones's wife, Susan. Fanny Barton, Jones's older sister, had three sons in Clark's company, although Robert, the "sickly one," was quickly discharged.

The Fifth Virginia Infantry was also filled with men who were either familiar to Jackson or would become familiar to him very soon. The regiment was commanded by Colonel Kenton Harper, mayor of Staunton, Virginia,

Members of the Marion Rifles, Company A, Fifth Virginia Infantry, in 1895. *Courtesy of WFCHS.*

and the militia "general" whom Jackson had replaced at Harpers Ferry when he took command. The Fifth had two companies from Winchester: the Marion Rifles, commanded by John Henry Stover Funk, and the Continental Morgan Guard, commanded by John Avis. Known to his friends as Stover, Funk was a recent graduate of the Winchester Medical School, where he studied under Hunter McGuire, and was practicing medicine in Marion County, Virginia, when the war began. Avis, like Botts, had gained distinction before the war as the sheriff of Jefferson County during the John Brown trial.

The Fourth Virginia Infantry had two companies from Jackson's hometown: the Rockbridge Grays and the Liberty Hall Volunteers, the latter made up of students from Washington College in Lexington. Although the Fourth Virginia Infantry had no companies from Winchester, the Valley town was well represented by Lieutenant Colonel Lewis T. Moore. The Winchester lawyer, who had probably met Jackson during the execution of John Brown in 1859 since Moore was there as colonel of the Thirty-first Virginia Militia, spent a great deal of time actually commanding the regiment; its commander, James Francis Preston, was in poor health and not

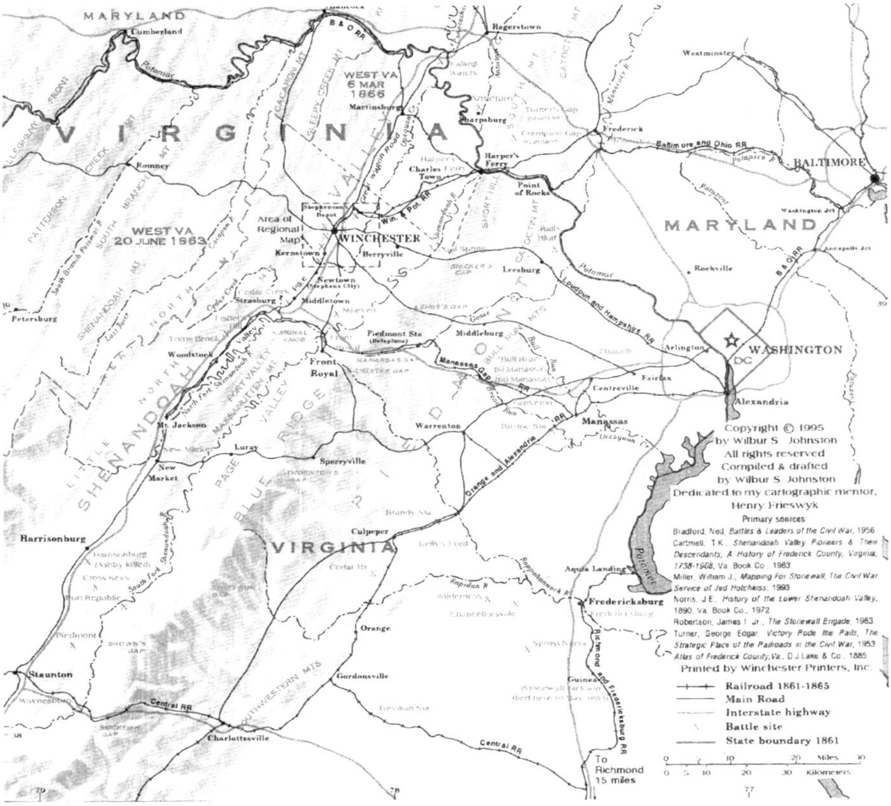

Shenandoah Valley during the Civil War. *Courtesy of Wilbur Johnston.*

able to perform his duties on a regular basis. In his mid-forties, Moore, most believed, was a fortunate choice for second in command since he possessed a maturity needed to supervise the young recruits.

The Twenty-seventh Virginia Infantry was the smallest of the infantry regiments in Jackson's new brigade, but in many ways it may have been the most familiar to him. The regiment was made up entirely of companies from the southern Valley, including Jackson's hometown of Lexington. Colonel John Echols, a graduate of Washington College in Lexington and Harvard Law School, was appointed commander of the regiment.

One member of the company known as the Allegheny Roughs was very familiar to Jackson. VMI graduate Joseph Carpenter had been one of Jackson's best artillery students at the institute. The Rockbridge Rifles hailed from Lexington and was commanded by Captain Samuel Letcher, brother of the governor. Another member of the company was Elisha Paxton. The Lexington lawyer was a neighbor and close personal friend of Jackson before the war.

The Rockbridge Artillery, however, was probably the closest to Jackson of the five units. The battery name, "Rockbridge," meant that the vast majority of its members were from the same county as Jackson. Commanded by William N. Pendleton, the four pieces of artillery in the battery, which Episcopal Pendleton nicknamed "Matthew, Luke, Mark and John," were the same field pieces that Jackson had used at VMI to instruct cadets during artillery drills.

One former VMI cadet and Winchester native who would soon join the battery was certainly well known to Jackson, although it is doubtful that Marshall Barton's former professor knew of his abilities as a poet. In 1855, while a student under Jackson at the institute, Barton wrote this barb:

Hickory, Alias Major T.J. Jackson

Like some rude brute that ranged the forest wild,
So rude, uncouth, so purely Nature's child,
Is "Hickory," and yet me thinks I see
The stamp of genius on his brow,
And he, with his wild glance and keen but quiet eye,
Can draw forth from the secret recesses where they lie
Those thoughts and feelings of the human heart.
Most virtuous, good and free from guilty art,
There is something in his very mode of life
So accurate, so steady, void of care or strife,
That fills my heart with love for him who bears his honor meekly,
And who wears the laurels of a hero.

2
"Let the Soldiers Go and You Stay Here!"

While Jackson worked to turn his new brigade into an effective fighting force, General Johnston dealt with the problem of defending Harpers Ferry. With Federal forces gathering all around him, he was deeply aware of the indefensibility of his position. Harpers Ferry was surrounded by heights and could be easily surrounded and captured. After repeated requests, he was finally given permission to abandon the post and move his command to a more defensible position. On June 13, he ordered a retreat to Bunker Hill, Virginia, just a few miles north of Winchester.

For the Winchester natives in Jackson's brigade, war must have seemed strangely wonderful. After marching off to fight, they had settled into their new role as soldiers under the watchful eye of their new commander. Now, after nearly two months of training and adjusting to living in tents or worse, they received an order they hardly expected. They were going home. Daniel Conrad, another Winchester resident in the brigade, described Jackson at this time:

> *Our senior colonel was a man who never spoke unless spoken to; never seemed to sleep. He walked about alone, the projecting visor of his blue cap concealing his features; a badly fitting, single breasted blue coat, and high boots covering the largest feet ever seen completed his picture. Cadets from the Virginia Military Institute, called him "Old Jack." He was as exact in the performance of his duties as a mathematical proposition.*

Jackson, however, strongly disagreed with the decision to retreat. Since the commencement of the war, he had urged offensive action and believed that

General Turner Ashby. *Courtesy of BR/GQ.*

if the troops at Harpers Ferry were to be moved, it should be into Maryland, not Bunker Hill. He kept his opinion to himself, though, and marched south with his brigade on June 16, reaching Bunker Hill two days later.

One Confederate soldier who was not retreating was Captain Turner Ashby. Born and raised in Markham, Virginia, Ashby, along with the rest of the Seventh Virginia Cavalry, was charged with screening Johnston's movements from Union forces just across the Potomac River near Williamsport, Maryland. Ashby was one of the foremost horsemen of the area; even at this early stage of the war, he was gaining a reputation for daring that was an inspiration to his fellow cavalrymen, and the young girls in the area were quickly becoming infatuated with him.

One feat even gained the attention of General Johnston. Disguised as a country doctor, Ashby had crossed the Potomac River and entered the camp of the Union army. There, he gathered an enormous amount of information, which he forwarded to Johnston. In a letter to Ashby, Johnston expressed his "cordial thanks" and assured him that the knowledge of the enemy Ashby had provided made him "sleep very soundly last night." He also promised to promote him to lieutenant colonel.

Ashby eventually got that promotion, but it was more due to lack of confidence in the Seventh Virginia Cavalry's commander, Angus McDonald. The people of Winchester greeted the promotion warmly. Ashby, besides becoming a great help to Johnston, was becoming the nineteenth-century equivalent of a matinee idol to the young girls in Winchester.

Events taking place west of town, however, would change Ashby's daring into searing rage. While involved in a small action just north of Romney, Ashby's younger brother, Richard, was seriously wounded and left on the field. When Ashby finally found his wounded brother, he was shocked. Richard had multiple wounds, indicating that Union soldiers had tormented him while he lay helpless on the field. When his brother died from those wounds soon after the engagement, Turner Ashby was filled with a fury that colored his actions for the rest of his short life.

Jackson and his brigade arrived at Bunker Hill with opposing goals. The brigade commander wished to use the time for drill and training and was also very interested in seeking the enemy and punishing him. His soldiers, however, were more interested in taking advantage of their nearness to Winchester. This was especially true of the three companies that came from the Valley town. To them, it was a time to visit families, get a good night's sleep in their own beds, eat home-cooked meals and visit their wives and children—or, for the bachelors, continue pursuing the young girls in town.

But the sudden arrival of five thousand soldiers descending on the town had more serious consequences than home-cooked meals or stealing a kiss from one of the girls. They also brought a near epidemic of illness that always accompanied large armies, particularly new ones. The town worked heroically to care for the thousands of sick soldiers by putting them up in hotels, warehouses, churches and private homes. Not only did many of Johnston's men die during this season of disease, but many townspeople did as well.

Jackson's solution to both of these problems was to keep his men busy and as far away from Winchester as possible. The situation in the Valley at this time gave him ample opportunities to put his brigade to good use. It would also dramatically demonstrate the opposing approaches to war that existed between him and his commander, General Johnston.

Johnston had correctly surmised that Winchester was the most important point for the Confederate army in the Northern Shenandoah Valley. The town protected Strasburg, where the Manassas Gap Railroad was the northernmost rail connection between the Valley and the rest of Virginia. For the Union forces under General Robert Patterson, the key point was Martinsburg, where the Baltimore and Ohio Railroad passed through the Valley. Martinsburg was also the site of an enormous amount of equipment and shops needed for the repair and maintenance of the railroad.

Frank and Susan Jones.
Courtesy of WFCHS.

In late June, Jackson and his brigade were assigned the task of destroying all of Martinsburg's shops, equipment and rolling stock. This order highlighted the basic disagreement between Jackson and Johnston on how to conduct the war. As the war progressed, Johnston became famous for abandoning key positions and destroying valuable supplies and equipment while retreating. Jackson, on the other hand, was well known for his reluctance to leave valuable supplies to the enemy, and it was believed that he would fight a battle over one broken wagon.

The operation at Martinsburg gave Jackson a chance to demonstrate this. He destroyed enough of the Martinsburg railroad shops to satisfy Johnston's orders; when the Union army finally occupied the town, it had been picked clean, and the railroad yard was in complete ruins. Jackson also saved forty locomotives, which he disassembled, placed on specially made flatbed wagons pulled by forty-horse teams and transported to Strasburg over the Valley Turnpike. There, they were reassembled and transported by the Manassas Gap Railroad for use in the rest of Virginia.

While defending the town during these operations, he was also able to draw the enemy into a battle near Falling Waters. It was the brigade's first taste of combat, and both the men and Jackson, who accompanied them, handled themselves well. He was not surprised with their performance, though. Just a month before the battle, Jackson had written to his wife that when marching toward the enemy, "they are so inspired as apparently to forget their fatigue of the march; and though some of them were suffering from hunger, this and other privations appeared to be forgotten." He added that they averaged about "three miles an hour," but in retreat, "their reluctance was manifested by their snail-like pace."

On the day Jackson returned from Martinsburg, there was a letter waiting for the colonel at Winchester. It read:

> *Richmond, Va., July 3, 1861.*
> *My dear general, I have the pleasure of sending you a commission of brigadier general in the Provisional Army, and to feel that you merit it. May your advancement increase your usefulness to the State,*
> *Yours truly,*
> *R.E. Lee*

The new general also had another addition to his brigade. On July 15, the Thirty-third Virginia Infantry was added to Jackson's brigade. It was commanded by Colonel Arthur Cummings, who graduated from VMI just a few years before Frank Jones. Jackson must have been glad to have the new regiment since his existing ones were at half strength due to the large number of sick soldiers in his command. Within the regiment was the Mountain Rangers, a company recruited from the mountainous regions in Frederick County to the west of Winchester. The men had elected young Frederick Holliday as their captain. Considered a rising legal star among the lawyers in his hometown of Winchester, he lived next door to the Bartons on Cameron Street.

Holliday exercised the same boldness that had gained him fame at the bar. The new company commander wrote a pointed letter to Frank Jones, the brother of his neighbor Mrs. Barton. Knowing that Jones was on Jackson's staff, he wrote, "My men want shoes badly. I applied to the Quartermaster in this place, and he informed me that he could not furnish them without the authority of Col. Jackson." He asked Jones to order them at once and reminded his friend, "My men want Minié Rifles, as it is a Rifle Company."

Poor Jones was overwhelmed not only by his normal duties under his very polite, but very demanding, new brigadier general but by his friends as well. As June turned into July, he did have the relief of knowing that his position

Robert Y. Conrad represented Winchester at the 1861 Virginia Secession Convention, where he led the fight to keep the state in the Union. Conrad was the unofficial leader of Winchester throughout the Civil War and a good friend of Stonewall Jackson. Conrad's five sons served in the Confederate army, and his daughter, Sallie Conrad, was Henry Kyd Douglas's unrequited love interest during the Civil War. *Courtesy of BR/GQ.*

on Jackson's staff was likely to be permanent. His letter home to his wife, Susan, left no doubt that he had very little confidence in her ability to run the farm in his absence, and letters to his mother put great stress on the need for her and his younger brother, Beverly, to go to the farm and make sure everything was done properly. But after he called on Beverly to drop everything and enlist, the reply was not from his wife but rather his mother.

Even though Frank Jones was in his early thirties, a college graduate, a husband and father, the owner of his own farm and an important officer on General Jackson's staff, he was still the son of Ann Cary Randolph Jones, and his mother had strong opinions about her family. Although her letter was filled with diplomatic tact and the sweetness that only a mother could pen, she reminded Frank that he had been pressing "Bev" to shear the sheep at his farm, even though his little brother was ill. Mrs. Jones assured Frank that Bev was now better and had completed his brother's assignment. More importantly to Mrs. Jones, though, was that Bev's wife, Rebecca, had just given birth to a son, whom they named Edward. Bev would be happy to join the army, but only after arranging for the care and safety of her new grandson and his mother. It should be noted that Beverly Jones enlisted in the Rockbridge Artillery, Frank's recommendation, on July 3, 1861.

Stonewall Jackson in his VMI uniform, which he wore during the early months of the war. *Courtesy of THL.*

The problems in the Jones family, as well as in many other families in Winchester and Frederick County, seemed small after word began to spread around town in mid-July that General Johnston was about to abandon Winchester. Since General Patterson's Union army was steadily approaching the town from the north, it seemed to many that the Valley army was now going to retreat once more without a fight and abandon them to the mercies of the enemy.

Many in town saw the move as cowardly, and that view was shared by at least some of the soldiers in Jackson's command. The Liberty Hall Volunteers, a company from Washington College, had been the special interest of many of the Winchester girls, and marching away from the enemy in front of their new girlfriends was humiliating. Frank Jones wrote to his wife that the order was received with "great disaffection amongst those who came from the Valley." Of course, they would later learn that they were marching to a battle, not abandoning Winchester. One of the newest members of Jackson's command, Captain Frederick Holliday, once he discovered this, must have been particularly upset. While his regiment was preparing to leave with the rest of Johnston's army, Holliday's company and Company I, the Rockbridge Confederates, were ordered to remain behind on detached duty. For the brilliant and aggressive young attorney, this must have been gallingly disappointing.

Jackson, who had advocated offensive actions for the last three months, agreed with them. As the troops marched south through downtown Winchester on July 18, Jackson was approached by several prominent local citizens led by Robert Y. Conrad, who was the father of four sons under his command. Conrad asked Jackson, "Are you going to take these Virginia boys away from here, and leave us to the horde of Yankees who are coming down upon us?"

Conrad's next remark also revealed the growing confidence and trust that the citizens of Winchester had in the former VMI professor: "Let the soldiers go and you stay here!" Jackson, who had deep respect for Conrad, answered sharply, "I am a soldier and obey orders." Hunter McGuire, who witnessed the exchange, commented years later that Jackson's face at the time "was more full of mental anguish and grief then I had ever seen in it before."

Despite their reservations, as the young men of Jackson's brigade marched through Winchester, a huge crowd gathered on both sides of the street waving flags and cheering. Few would have guessed that among those 2,600 young men, 8 would eventually rise to the rank of general in the Confederate army.

General Joseph E. Johnston.
Courtesy of the National Archives.

Their reserved but demanding commander had trained them as well as any troops marching off to war, and all were determined to do their duty.

Still, the crowd had mixed emotions about this march through town. Many of the young girls in the audience had never received the kind of attention that accompanied the influx of thousands of soldiers to their small town. Would their new soldier boyfriends find someone more appealing elsewhere? The more mature in the crowd sensed that the boys were marching toward danger and strained to find their loved ones, hoping that it would not be the last time they ever saw them.

It was true that for many, this march would be their last. What none would have ever dreamed, though, was that these Valley men were marching toward a place called Manassas and an insignificant local landmark named Henry House Hill. There, they and their professor general would find immortality.

3
"I Don't Remember to Have Ever Seen More Beautiful Papering"

What happened on July 21, 1861, is one of the most told stories of the war. With the battle seemingly lost and the Confederate army in disarray after a flank attack by General Irvin McDowell's Union army, Jackson and his brigade stabilized the Confederate line on Henry House Hill and turned the tide of the battle. General Bernard Bee, in an attempt to rally the retreating Confederate soldiers, looked to Jackson's brigade and shouted, "There stands Jackson like a stonewall; rally around the Virginians!"

Bee's statement caught fire in the Southern press, and Jackson and his brigade became known from that point forward as "Stonewall" Jackson and the "Stonewall Brigade." Like in all battles, though, the new nickname and the immortality that came with it were purchased at a heavy price. Many, including General Bee, had fought their last battles and lay dead upon the field. The official count shows that 16 percent of Jackson's brigade became casualties during the battle. Winchester, along with the rest of the Valley, was no exception to the price, and the bodies of five members of the brigade arrived in the Valley town a few days later for burial.

Several of the local men were wounded and had missed death by the barest of margins. Even Jackson had not escaped and was wounded painfully in the finger. If not for the timely appearance of Dr. McGuire, the finger would have been amputated on the field. Frank Jones had been spared, but his brother-in-law, Captain William L. Clark, was badly wounded and would never fight again with the brigade. Several other close relatives had close calls. Randolph and Strother Barton, sons of Frank's older sister, were both wounded, and Tom Marshall, the widower of Frank's late niece, had his horse shot from under him.

Lieutenant Colonel Lewis T. Moore, Fourth Virginia Infantry, offered his home on Peyton Street to Stonewall Jackson in the fall of 1861 as a headquarters and home. *Courtesy of BR/GQ.*

Perhaps the most lamented loss was Lieutenant Colonel Lewis T. Moore of the Fourth Virginia Infantry. Moore had performed brilliantly with his regiment from its first days around Harpers Ferry through the Battle of Manassas. Both Moore and the Fourth's commander, Colonel Preston, received serious wounds. Moore had his knee shattered by a bullet and would remain crippled for the rest of his life. Although he was much older than most of his soldiers and was the victim at times of good-natured teasing, the men of his regiment would miss him sorely.

Years after the war, his men described him as "brave, but not reckless. Honest, sturdy, kindhearted, charitable, he was one of God's noblemen, and, was never known to turn a deaf ear to distress when able to alleviate it, nor did he ever fail to respond when duty called him." Just as importantly, Jackson had great faith in Moore's abilities from his first day at Harpers Ferry. The wound was so serious that, for a while, many in his command were concerned that he might not survive.

While the brigade was licking its wounds and enjoying its new notoriety, Jackson's patience with defensive warfare was growing thin. While at a hospital having his injured finger treated after the battle, he came upon the Confederate president, Jefferson Davis. Within hearing distance of Davis, Jackson lashed out, "Give me 10,000 men and I'll take Washington tomorrow!" The problem was that the green Confederate army was almost as disorganized in victory as was the Union army in defeat, and no attempt to take the Union capital was attempted.

Although he was known for his stiffness, poor appearance and never joining in conversation with the officers around Johnston, Jackson was more open with ministers who visited his camp and especially with his wife. He even, on one occasion, indulged in a little humor. When his wife complained shortly after the battle that his achievements were not getting enough attention in the press, he reminded her, "I am glad that the battle was fought on your birthday so you can never tell me any more that I forget your birthday. See if I don't always remember it, though I do not my own."

With both armies inactive and unlikely to become active any time soon, Jackson was able to bring his wife to his camp from North Carolina, where she was staying with her family. Although the young couple enjoyed their time together, it was shortened by the closeness of two armies and the need to keep vigilant. After her departure, both looked forward to a time in the future when they could reunite.

Front entrance of the Moore house, which was purchased by Lieutenant Colonel Lewis T. Moore in 1856 and used by Stonewall Jackson as a home and headquarters between November 1861 and March 1862. *Courtesy of BR/GQ.*

While stationed near Manassas, Jackson's positions on the proper role of the army were causing difficulties in the weeks and months after the battle. He and his brigade were now national celebrities, and his words, even if spoken in private, were likely to end up in newspaper headlines all over the South. Jackson's innate modesty minimized the damage, but it was common knowledge throughout the Confederacy what was his position. When President Davis visited the army in the fall, he and Jackson got into a sharp debate over what to do in northwestern Virginia. When the president seemed to show no interest in offensive operations in the area and simply assumed that it was a Union stronghold, Jackson was furious.

Fortunately for Jackson and the Confederate cause, another problem was brewing that would satisfy both Jackson and the authorities in Richmond, who were weary of his suggestions for bold offensive operations. The situation in the Shenandoah Valley, and Winchester in particular, was growing desperate by the day, and citizens in the area were demanding that the Confederate authorities in Richmond do something about it.

The problem was that the town was protected by militia and the Seventh Virginia Cavalry, still under the command of Colonel Angus McDonald.

The Taylor Hotel in 1889. Owned by Lewis T. Moore during the Civil War, it was Stonewall Jackson's first headquarters in Winchester and where he met his wife at midnight on Christmas Eve 1861, when she arrived from North Carolina. *Courtesy of WFCHS.*

Citizens considered McDonald to be woefully incompetent, and the militia officers had little or no control over their men. Complaints were registered over the number of women in the Confederate camps outside town. One local paper asked, "Where do so many come from?" No one suggested that the large number of women in these camps were the wives of the soldiers. With a Union army training just across the Potomac River, few believed that this assortment of militia units was in a position to put up any resistance.

Another problem was one that would plague the Valley town throughout the war. Nearly all the public buildings and many private residences were filled to capacity with sick soldiers. A committee led by Robert Y. Conrad wrote to Jackson on September 15, "Our town is now suffering intolerably from the army under your command and unless some remedy is immediately applied we have reason to apprehend the most serious consequences of pestilences and famine." They found that the soldiers protecting the town "had for some time become a great nuisance."

The complaints were not just coming from Winchester. Other counties in the northern Valley were having the same problem. They complained, "We have plenty of men ready and willing to protect the border, [but] we are suffering needlessly for want of competent officers." To the west of Winchester, Union Generals Lander and Kelley were conducting a successful campaign near Romney that would eventually affect the northern Valley. With a very real threat only miles away and the citizens of Winchester and the rest of the northern Valley desperately in need of help, Richmond decided to act in the one way that would satisfy everyone.

Jackson, who had received a promotion to major general on October 7, 1861, was informed on October 23, in a long letter from Secretary of State Judah Benjamin, that he was to receive command of the Shenandoah Valley with his headquarters in Winchester. The formal order, however, did not arrive at General Johnston's headquarters until October 28. Hoping to retain Jackson, Johnston held back the letter for a couple days, but on November 4, he forwarded the orders to Jackson. The new major general had been packed for days.

The order was issued for two reasons. The clamor coming from the northern Shenandoah Valley for protection always insisted that Jackson be the one appointed. This order would satisfy their demands. But another reason lurked in the background. Jackson's strong—and to Richmond, radical—stance on offensive warfare was unwelcome in the capital, and Richmond authorities believed that this new command would keep Jackson too busy to cause any more trouble.

There was only one more act to complete before Jackson boarded a train for Winchester, and it was an exceedingly painful one. His assignment to Winchester did not include the Stonewall Brigade. At 1:00 p.m. on November 4, Jackson did something he rarely did: he gave a speech. Assembling the brigade, the men's former commander spoke with an emotion that left everyone in tears, including Jackson. Many members of the brigade quietly vowed to follow the general wherever he went and were seriously considering leaving for the Valley without orders.

Another consequence of Jackson's new assignment was the reshuffling of his staff. Only chief of staff Colonel John T.L. Preston and aide "Sandie" Pendleton would accompany Jackson to Winchester. Frank Jones, now a captain on Jackson's staff, resigned, believing that with his larger responsibilities, Jackson had the right to pick whomever he wanted. It was the last time Jones would serve on Jackson's staff officially, although he would serve in that capacity at least one more time unofficially. Jones resignation, though, resulted in a promotion to major and assignment to the Second Virginia Infantry, reuniting him with his VMI classmates James Allen and Lawson Botts, who were the colonel and lieutenant colonel, respectively, of the regiment.

Mary Anna Jackson, Stonewall Jackson's second wife. *Courtesy of Preston Library, VMI.*

Leaving immediately after addressing his brigade, Jackson's was a quiet journey from Manassas to the Valley on the Manassas Gap Railroad. After arriving at Strasburg late in the day, Jackson, along with Preston and Pendleton, immediately made the eighteen-mile journey to Winchester on horseback. Their arrival was without any fanfare. Checking into the Taylor Hotel on Loudoun Street, which was owned by Lieutenant Colonel Lewis T. Moore, Jackson and his party went immediately to bed.

While Jackson and his two staff officers slept, his arrival caused quite a stir. When the trio awoke the next morning, there was a throng of people outside the hotel to greet and speak to him. Jackson turned down all requests for an audience, and he, Preston and Pendleton went to work on surveying the situation in his new command. What they found was that the situation in the northern Valley was even grimmer than they had expected. The town was overrun with sick soldiers, and the militia was a poorly armed, undisciplined mob.

The only infantrymen in the area were three militia "brigades," two scattered cavalry commands and no artillery. Jackson met with Turner Ashby within a few days after arriving, and the new commander of the Seventh Virginia Cavalry came away from the meeting pleased with his new leader. Jackson also sent Colonel Preston to Richmond to ask for reinforcements.

Dr. James R. Graham, pastor of the Kent Street Presbyterian Church, where Stonewall Jackson attended services while he was in Winchester. Photo taken in 1895. *Courtesy of WFCHS.*

One thing Jackson must have done before he left was to request that the Stonewall Brigade be sent to the Valley. On the day after his arrival in Winchester, the brigade was ordered to report to Jackson.

The brigade's trip to the Valley was anything but in keeping with Jackson's strong beliefs concerning the proper conduct of soldiers. His old brigade, along with the Rockbridge Artillery, was so excited about joining its old commander that most arrived in Winchester drunk. One of the regiments arrived with only two hundred men. The rest were somewhere in between Manassas and Winchester in a state of inebriation.

Another problem Jackson faced in his first days in Winchester was the need to move his headquarters from the Taylor Hotel to some place less public. Located in downtown Winchester, the hotel offered very little privacy, as townspeople flocked to see the hero of Manassas. Fortunately, a solution to the problem came quickly from his wounded colleague, Lieutenant Colonel Lewis T. Moore.

Moore, a bachelor, was recovering from his wound in Richmond, and his six-room home on Peyton Street, several blocks north of town, was empty. Built in 1854 by Dr. William Fuller, Moore had purchased the house in 1856. When Moore learned that Jackson needed a headquarters, he kindly offered the house as both a home and a headquarters. The general, delighted with its location and accommodations, accepted.

Besides offering the general a quiet place away from downtown, the Moore house was also conveniently located just a few doors down from the Kent Street Presbyterian Manse, occupied by Dr. James R. Graham and his wife, Fanny. Although constantly involved in the war effort from its very beginning, Jackson never forgot his obligations as a Christian. He was regularly visited by ministers, including his pastor from Lexington, while at Manassas, and he regularly sent his tithe home after receiving his pay. Now in Winchester, one of his first duties was to find a church home.

The Presbyterian Church in Winchester had split several years before the war over a conflict concerning evangelism. The Kent Street Church was founded in 1827 and in 1851 had hired Dr. Graham as its pastor. Although Jackson was as strict a Presbyterian as could be found anywhere, he was not a strong believer in predestination and was heavily involved in evangelism from his first day as a new member of the denomination. Since the Kent Street Church was founded with evangelism in mind, Jackson was drawn to that church, where he quickly became close friends with Dr. Graham.

Now that he was settled in a new home and headquarters and had found a church home, Jackson's next priority was to bring his wife to Winchester. Mary Anna, after her brief stay at Manassas, had returned to North Carolina.

With winter approaching and the likelihood of any aggressive movements by the enemy small, his first campaign as the new commander of the Valley District was to bring Mary Anna to his side. A little over a week after arriving in Winchester, he began that campaign:

> *You can have plenty of society of charming ladies here, and the Rev. Mr. Graham, our Presbyterian minister, lives in the second house from here. This house belongs to Lieutenant-Colonel Moore, and has a large yard around it. The situation is beautiful. The building is of cottage style and contains six rooms. I have two rooms, one above the other. My lower room, or office, has a matting on the floor, a large fine table, six chairs, and a piano. The walls are papered with elegant gilt paper. I don't remember to have ever seen more beautiful papering, and there are five paintings hanging on the wall. If I only had my little woman here, the room would be set off. Through the blessing of our ever-kind Heavenly Father, I am quite comfortable. I have much work to perform, and wouldn't have much time to talk to my darling except at night: but then there is so much pleasant society among the ladies here that you could pass your time very agreeably.*

After receiving the letter, Mrs. Jackson left "without waiting for the promised 'aide' to be sent." Finding several friends who were going to Richmond, she joined them. Finding a minister there who agreed to escort her, she traveled to Strasburg by rail and from there by stagecoach. During her journey from Strasburg, she was informed that General Jackson was away from Winchester: "It was with a feeling of sad disappointment and loneliness that that I alighted from the stage-coach in front of the Taylor's Hotel at midnight."

Walking up the stairs to the hotel entrance, she noticed several officers lurking in the shadows and standing on the sidewalk. "Just before reaching the landing, I turned to look back, for one figure among the group looked startlingly familiar. But he had not come forward." She did notice an officer "in a military overcoat, and cap drawn down over his eyes, following us in rapid pursuit." By the time she reached the top of the stairs, this officer's "strong arms caught me in the rear." Suddenly, she was being "kissed and kissed over again" before she realized that the officer was Jackson.

She also recorded that her elderly minister escort "chuckled gleefully" at the encounter. When Mrs. Jackson asked her husband why he had delayed in greeting her, the general replied coyly that "he wanted to assure himself that it was his own wife, as he didn't want to commit the blunder of kissing anybody else's *esposa*."

4
"A Special Kindness to Her and Myself"

With the arrival of Mary Anna Jackson in Winchester began one of the best periods of their short marriage. There, they made many friendships that were cherished by both the general and his wife. But it was also the beginning of a period filled with controversy that eventually took Jackson from being the hero of Manassas to becoming one of the great captains of American history. For the people of Winchester, Jackson and the Stonewall Brigade's return was a gift from heaven. Located just thirty miles from the Potomac River, they lived in fear of Union occupation from the early weeks of the war. The Winchester Unionist diarist Julia Chase, who would grow to despise Jackson, dryly commented on November 9, 1861, "Our town is all astir in consequence of the arrival of Jackson's Brigade. The citizens feel perfectly safe now, I suppose."

The *Winchester Republican*, a pro-Confederate paper, stated in mid-December, "This distinguished officer, now in command of the Valley District of Virginia, has perhaps as great a hold upon the confidence, admiration and respect of the people as any officer in the Confederate service." Robert Y. Conrad, even before the arrival of the Stonewall Brigade, wrote to his son Holmes, "The return here of Jackson has had a great effect upon the spirits of our citizens. Although unattended by men or officers, his coming has inspired confidence in our safety."

After settling in with his wife and staff at the Moore House, Jackson quickly went to work to ready his small army for offensive operations. One of his first orders was that neither officers nor enlisted men were allowed in Winchester for any reason other than official business. This did not sit well

Fanny Magill Graham, wife of Dr. James Graham, pastor of the Kent Street Presbyterian Church, and sister of Mary Tucker Magill. She became Mary Anna Jackson's closest friend while living in the Grahams' home on Braddock Street. *Courtesy of BR/GQ.*

with his old brigade, since many of its members were from Winchester and were camped only a few miles from home. Those orders were universally ignored, and he issued a sharp reprimand, singling out two regimental commanders for negligence of duty. One was Colonel Allen, who was temporarily commanding the Stonewall Brigade.

Another officer who would soon be assigned to Jackson's command and would become embroiled in controversy was Colonel William B. Taliaferro. Having met Jackson while serving on the Visitorial Board of VMI, he saw Jackson as "a man of peculiarities, quite distinctly marked from other people—reserved, yet polite; reticent of opinions, but fixed in the ideas he had formed." Taliaferro went on to say that Jackson never tried to force his views on others but was "determined and unflinching in their advocacy when pressed to any expression of them."

That firmness was tested almost immediately upon his arrival in Winchester. A private in the Seventh Virginia Cavalry, James A. Miller had shot his company commander, Captain John Henderson, after he arrested one of Miller's friends during a drunken binge. The bullet shattered Henderson's elbow and permanently paralyzed his right arm. A court-martial sentenced Miller to death by firing squad for the incident.

After the court-martial, Colonel John Preston, Jackson's chief of staff, asked Dr. James Graham to visit young Miller to see if the sentence could be reduced. After visiting with Miller, Graham said Miller told his story "with touching simplicity and candor." Graham also continued that Miller "deplored the hardship his execution would inflict upon his loss of reputation, and upon his helpless family in depriving them of protection and support." Graham also stated, "My sympathies were thoroughly enlisted, and nothing within my power was left undone to secure his pardon."

Miller could not have obtained two more powerful advocates than Graham and Preston. Jackson and Preston had attended Graham's church since their first Sunday in Winchester, and the trio were fast friends. Preston's wife, Maggie, was also the sister of Jackson's first wife. Since his conversion, Jackson considered his minister his "commanding officer" in Christian matters, and it was to Maggie that he turned for comfort when his first wife died suddenly while giving birth to a stillborn son.

When Graham and a friend visited Jackson to plead for clemency, "He [Jackson] listened with evident sympathy. His voice quivered, and there was moisture in his eyes." The general was particularly affected when Graham mentioned that Miller wished "to die as a soldier on the field of battle, and not as a dog at the muzzles of the muskets of his own comrades." Jackson was so overcome by Graham's pleas that he suggested several things that might be done for Miller.

Despite the powerful advocacy of Graham and Preston, Jackson still warned, "In this war we contend against fearful odds. Our soldiers are brave, but undisciplined; and discipline is essential to success. In an army, resistance to lawful authority is a grave offense. To pardon it would be to encourage insubordination and ruin our cause."

On November 24, 1861, Miller was executed by firing squad. By that time, however, the entire town, and particularly the other ministers, had heard Miller's story and Jackson's reply. The pastor of Market Street Methodist Church, Benjamin Brooke, had also interceded on Miller's behalf and recorded in his journal, "Baptized James Miller and attended to him at his execution." Brooke stated that Jackson suggested a petition be sent to Jefferson Davis, and that Davis sign it, but it was not delivered in time because the messenger "became intoxicated and did not return to Winchester until after the execution." According to Brooke, no one in town blamed Jackson for Miller's demise. They did turn their fury toward "L.B," whom Brooke identified as the drunken messenger. Brooke's final comment on the incident was that after "L.B." returned from Richmond, "he was met by a committee of infuriated citizens and warned to leave town immediately."

Despite Graham's failure to save Miller's life, his friendship with Jackson flourished. Preston, after less than a week in Winchester, wrote to Maggie,

The Kent Street Presbyterian Manse as it looks today. *Courtesy of BR/GQ.*

"We heard a most excellent Gospel sermon, preached with sincerity and fervor, from Mr. Graham of the Old School." Later in the day, Preston heard a sermon from the "New School" preached by a Dr. S.: "I did not relish the discourse. The house was crowded to suffocation, so I fell into a drowsy intellectual inanition that was painful." The "we" in Preston's letter referred to General and Mrs. Stonewall Jackson. Whether the Jacksons were also induced by "Dr. S." into "intellectual inanition," Preston did not say. The couple was, however, developing a close relationship with the Grahams and, through them, several other families in town.

The Grahams and the Jacksons were nearly the same age and had similar views on Christianity. James Graham had just turned thirty-six when the Jacksons moved into the Moore house, and Graham's wife, Fanny, was thirty-three, just a couple years older than Mary Anna. There was one important difference between the two couples, though. Living in the Graham home were three small children ranging in age from one to three, while the Jacksons were childless.

Although Jackson loved children and wanted one desperately, he was also terrified at the prospect. In less than a decade, he had lost a son,

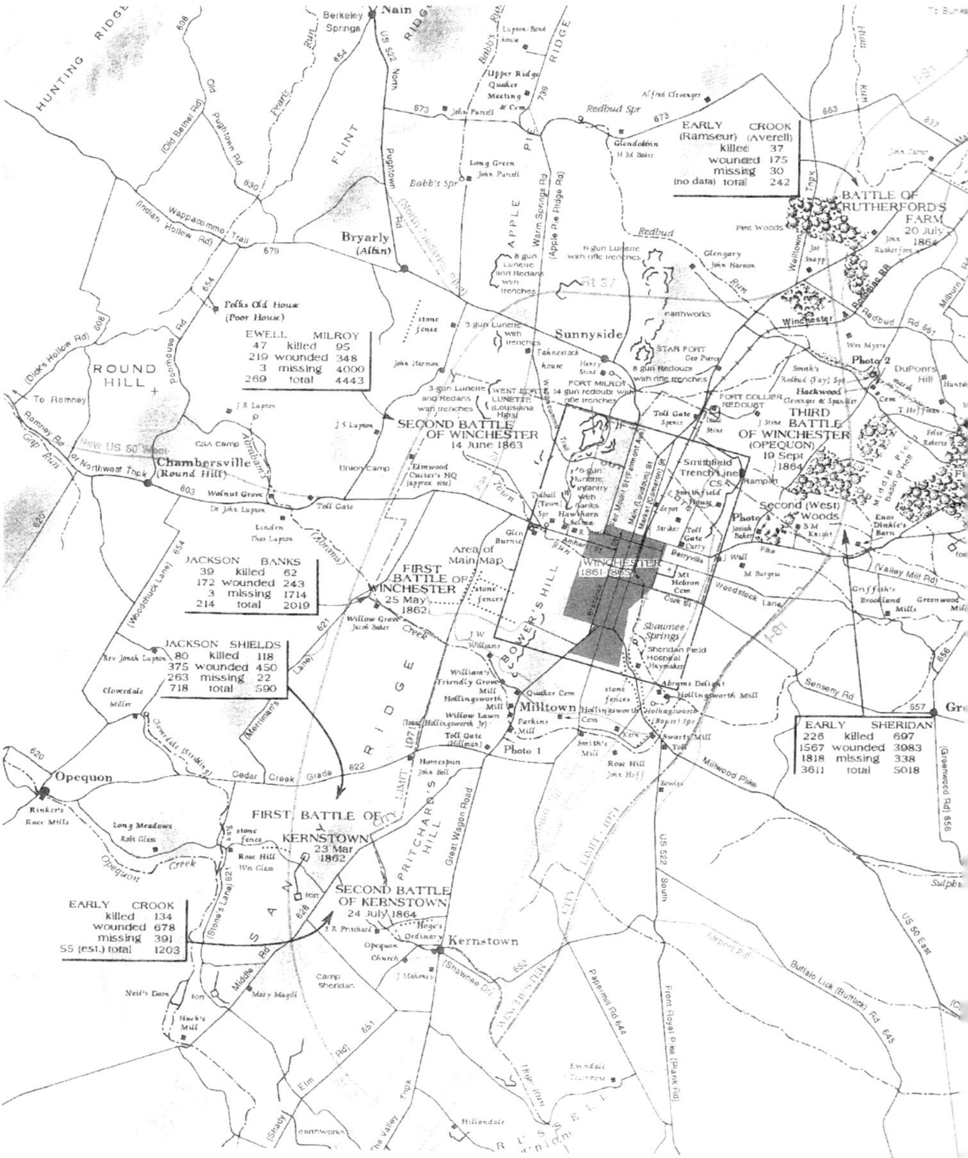

a daughter and a wife trying to have a baby. Mary Anna, however, did not share his fear, and one of her primary reasons for journeying to Winchester was to do something about it. Like her general husband, when it came to making a happy home, she firmly believed in offensive warfare.

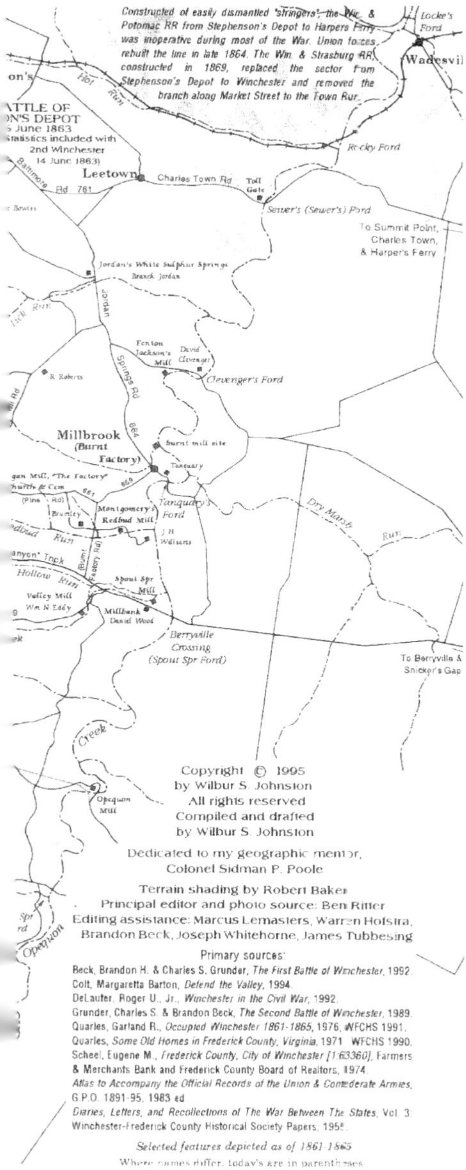

Map of Frederick County during the Civil War, including the location of all the battles fought in the county. *Courtesy of Wilbur Johnston.*

Mary Anna faced difficult odds since the Moore house was usually filled with soldiers. Jackson was straining every nerve to find a way to take the war to the enemy. One innovation that he made was to convert one of his infantry companies into an artillery battery. When Joseph Carpenter was promoted to captain of Company A, Twenty-seventh Virginia Infantry,

Jackson remembered what an excellent student of artillery he had been at VMI. He immediately converted Carpenter's infantry company into Carpenter's Battery.

Jackson also had his eye on damaging the C&O Canal that carried coal and wheat from the Midwest to the East Coast. In mid-December, he sent a detachment to the Potomac River to destroy Dam No. 5, in hopes of stopping the flow of supplies from the canal to Washington. Freezing weather and stout resistance by the Union soldiers guarding the dam prevented Jackson from doing much damage, and his Stonewall Brigade returned to Winchester, from what they referred to as "That Dam Expedition," to await Jackson's next excursion. Just before the attempt to destroy the dam, the War Department appointed General Richard Garnett to command the Stonewall Brigade. Garnett immediately found himself in an almost impossible situation.

Whoever replaced Jackson as commander of the Stonewall Brigade would suffer by comparison, but Garnett also hailed from the aristocratic society east of the Blue Ridge. The resentment between the Lutherans, Presbyterians and Methodists from the Shenandoah Valley and their Anglican neighbors east of the Blue Ridge was deep and had existed since the colonial period. Whether this played a part in the tensions that existed almost immediately between Garnett and the brigade is impossible to gauge. One thing, however, was certain: Jackson did not like Garnett from the moment he was assigned to command.

Despite the lack of success at Dam No. 5, Jackson was still determined to take the war to the enemy. His objective now was Romney, just thirty miles west of Winchester. The liberation of northwestern Virginia had always been close to Jackson's heart, and the capture of Romney, he believed, was the first step toward that goal. The town also offered an even better place to disrupt Union shipping on the C&O Canal and the B&O Railroad. With sickness also ravaging his command, he believed, like Napoleon, that a winter campaign would improve the health of his men.

After repeated requests to Richmond for reinforcements and approval of his plan, Jackson received permission for the campaign to commence, and General William Loring's small division was ordered to Winchester as reinforcements. After repeated delays, the last of Loring's men finally arrived in Winchester on December 27. With his army now at full strength, Jackson decided to move on January 1, 1862. There was now just one more arrangement to be made.

Early on the morning of January 1, 1862, Jackson showed up at the front door of 319 North Braddock Street. It was the location of the Kent Street

Presbyterian Manse and the home of James and Fanny Graham. Jackson had a request to make. "He asked us, as a great favor, to receive Mrs. Jackson, and take care of her for a few days, while he was absent from town, urging the fact, that she was a stranger here, was herself the daughter of a minster, and that it would be a special kindness both to her and to himself, if we would consent," Graham said.

The Grahams were, of course, delighted to have Mary Anna as their house guest. Graham continued, "Within an hour he had brought her to us, taken his leave and with his staff was following his army to Bath." While Mary Anna settled in with the Grahams, Jackson rode to catch up with his command on an unusually warm winter day. The rest of the month, however, proved to be anything but balmy.

For the next month, Jackson and his army battled brutal winter weather and, at times, stiff Union resistance. His first objective was Bath (now Berkeley Spring), and with his arrival near the small town, a series of setbacks ensued that tested Jackson's resolve and damaged his relationship with one of his closest friends.

While preparing for an assault on the small force guarding Bath, Colonel William Gilham, in command of a small brigade of Loring's command, was ordered by Loring to stop and put his command in camp. Jackson, however, blamed Gilham and was determined to have him sacked from the army. The amazing thing about the entire incident was that Gilham, an 1840 graduate of West Point and a professor at VMI, was probably Jackson's closest friend in Lexington. Friendship, however, had no place in Jackson's mind where duty was involved. Fortunately for all concerned, Gilham had earlier applied for transfer back to VMI, and his request was accepted, avoiding an ugly court-martial.

Through the next few weeks, Jackson and his command battled through snowstorms, sleet, poor logistics and broken-down horses but still eventually captured Romney. The cost, however, was enormous. Nearly half of the men in his small army were in hospitals in Winchester, either sick or completely broken down. In Romney, fistfights broke out between the Stonewall Brigade, which Loring's men called "Jackson's pet lambs," and the rest of Jackson's command. When Jackson ordered the Stonewall Brigade back to Winchester, leaving Loring's men in Romney to occupy the town, a near mutiny broke out.

Jackson's campaign, although a modest success, left his reputation at the lowest point in his career. Through February 1862, the Confederacy had experienced almost nothing but success, and many in Richmond saw Jackson's Romney Campaign as a fool's errand. In Romney, a cabal also was forming among the officers in Loring's command who challenged Jackson's leadership and competence, and Richmond was listening sympathetically to their complaints. Outside of his friends in Winchester, most believed Jackson was a fanatic.

Shortly after Jackson returned to Winchester, a group of officers in Romney approached Loring with a request that a protest of their situation be sent to Richmond requesting that Loring's command be moved to Winchester. After Secretary of War Judah Benjamin received these officers, led by Colonel William Taliaferro, he sent a letter to Jackson in Winchester ordering Loring's command to be returned to Winchester. Jackson replied with the following letter:

> *Hon. J.P. Benjamin, Secretary of War, Sir:*
> *Your order requiring me to direct General Loring to return with his command to Winchester immediately has been received and promptly complied with.*
> *With such interference in my command I cannot expect to be of much service in the field; and accordingly respectfully request to be ordered to report for duty to the Superintendent of the Virginia Military Institute at Lexington; as has been done in the case of other Professors. Should this application not be granted, I respectfully request that the President will accept my resignation from the Army.*
> *I am, very respectfully, your obedient servant, T.J. Jackson.*

Jackson's religious convictions did not allow him to participate in either gambling or card playing, but if he had been so inclined, his letter to Benjamin proved that he had the instincts of a master poker player. When news of Jackson's resignation became known in Winchester, it caused a panic that spread throughout the northern Shenandoah Valley. It had nearly the same effect in Richmond, where Benjamin, an astute politician but no military man, was shocked. The only person who did not seem to be upset was Jackson.

Since his return from Romney, Jackson was staying at the Grahams' home with his wife. After receiving the directive from Benjamin, he had left for his headquarters at the Moore house, wrote his letter of resignation and returned to the Grahams' for breakfast. When his hosts noticed that he was late, and that Mary Anna, who usually accompanied him, was not with him, Jackson apologized and remarked, "Mrs. Jackson is a good deal disconcerted by the change we have decided upon. We expect soon to return to our home in Lexington."

When Jackson stated that Loring was being recalled from Romney, Graham immediately assumed that a large Union force was threatening the town. Jackson assured him that was not the case and explained the situation.

Graham was furious, but Jackson did not appear "to be ruffled in the least. His tones were just as even, his words as calm, his language as free from asperity, and his whole manner as thoroughly composed as I had ever known him."

As Graham's temper rose, Jackson explained, "If they have not confidence in my ability to administer wisely the affairs of this district, it is their duty to try to repair the damage they believe I am doing." The Presbyterian minister was surprised at Jackson's "meek, unselfish, unresentful spirit." While Jackson stoically prepared to return with his wife to their home in Lexington, Winchester and the rest of the northern Shenandoah Valley began taking actions they hoped would keep the man they had come to respect and depend on at his post.

5
"He Was Not Asleep"

One of Jackson's strongest supporters in the army admitted to the horror that was the Romney Campaign. Writing to his mother on January 6, 1862, Major Frank Jones admitted, "I have never in my life gone through as much suffering & as much exposure, as we have done on this trip. Wednesday night we slept on Sleeping Giant Mountain without our blankets & with nothing to eat, our wagons did not get up with us until late the next day."

Back home in early February, after referring to his camp north of Winchester as a "gloomy place," Jones told his mother, "Romney is evacuated. So is Bath. Genl. Jackson has resigned I declare I believe the world is turned upside down." It was a feeling held by most of the men camped around the young major. Winchester reeled from the shock that their protector was leaving the army. Henry Kyd Douglas, who was serving as an aide on Jackson's staff, commented on the women of Winchester: "In many parlors harsh words escaped fair lips, little fists were clenched, and bright eyes flashed at the treatment of their General."

But ill feelings were not just found in the Valley town; the revulsion to Benjamin's action had even stirred the anger of Jackson's commanding officer at Manassas, General Joseph E. Johnston. Johnston held back the resignation a couple days, hoping he could change Jackson's mind. When that failed, he forwarded the resignation with the observation: "I don't know how the loss of this officer can be supplied." He also caustically remarked in his forwarding letter, "Respectfully referred to the Secretary of War, whose orders I cannot countermand."

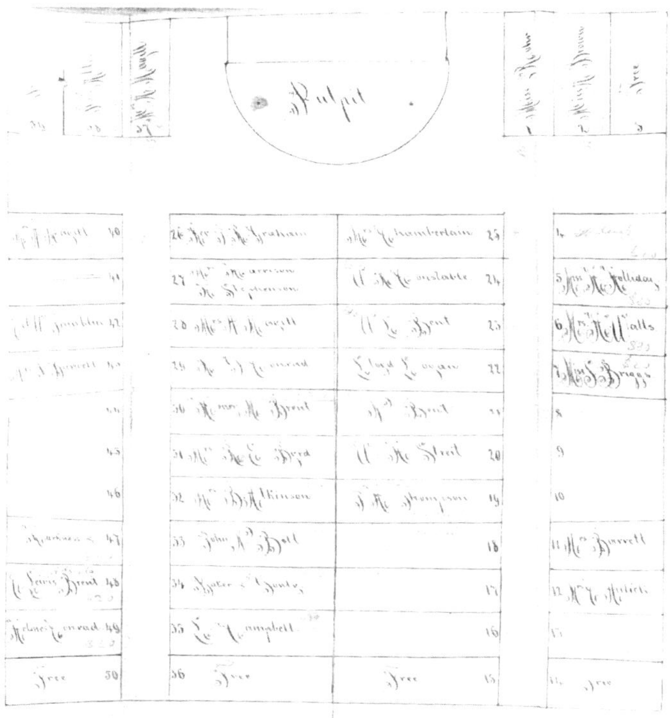

Pew designation for the Kent Street Presbyterian Church during the Civil War. *Courtesy of WFCHS.*

When Confederate congressman Alexander Boteler from Shepherdstown received a copy of the resignation, he stormed over to President Davis's office and showed it to him. Davis's first response was to refuse to accept it. While Davis stewed on the problem, Boteler went to see one of Jackson's closest friends and his neighbor in Lexington, Governor John Letcher.

Upon seeing the resignation and learning why it had been sent, Letcher flew into a towering rage. He immediately went to Benjamin's office at the War Department. After convincing Benjamin to delay acting on the letter until he had a chance to appeal to Jackson, Letcher stormed out. When he heard a clerk remark that "Jackson is a crazy man," Letcher responded with some heat, "It's a damned pity that Jackson's character or insanity does not attack some in this department."

With the uproar, Jackson began to receive letters from several sources imploring him to reconsider. One such letter was delivered to Jackson by Boteler. It was from the governor. After receiving the appeal from Letcher, Jackson and Boteler sat down to supper and debated what action Jackson should take. Appealing to his sense of duty to his state and his men,

Letcher assured him that one result of his letter was that Benjamin was as worried as anyone and that this type of directive would never come from his office again.

Boteler's appeals had the desired effect, and Jackson withdrew his resignation. The only result of the encounter was the removal of all regiments in Jackson's district that were not from Virginia. That dangerously reduced the forces needed to defend Winchester and the northern Shenandoah Valley. People in town, however, took very little notice and were greatly relieved to know that their favorite general was staying.

While Jackson's campaign to capture Romney, thanks to horrible weather and interference from Richmond, had proved a failure, Mary Anna's campaign to provide her general husband with a baby took a decided turn toward victory. Mrs. Jackson, with all the soldiers about, had found the Moore house a poor place to wage her campaign, and after Jackson returned from the Romney Campaign, instead of having her move back to his headquarters, he moved in with the Grahams.

The Grahams lived at 319 North Braddock Street, just a block from the Moore house. Dr. Graham and his wife, Fanny, had three young children, a daughter who was five, a three-year-old son and the youngest, also a boy, a year and a half. Jackson seemed to gravitate toward the middle son, Alfred. Fanny was the daughter of Anne Tucker Magill, whose home was

Dr. Hugh McGuire, founder of the Winchester Medical College and father of Dr. Hunter McGuire. *Courtesy of BR/GQ.*

Mary Tucker Magill, famed postwar author and close friend of Stonewall Jackson during the war. *Courtesy of THL.*

at 418 North Loudoun Street, just two blocks away. A widow, Anne lived with Fanny's younger sister, Mary Tucker Magill. All three were fiercely Confederate and would become fast friends with the Jacksons during their stay in Winchester.

The Jacksons took many meals at the Magill house and were deeply impressed with Fanny's mother. Anne was considered a great wit and one of the most sought-after hostesses in town. Mary Anna observed that "this family seemed to possess as an inheritance the richest vein of humor, in addition to high mental endowments. It would be difficult to describe the sunshine, which irradiated the very presence as well as the whole life of Mrs. Magill."

Both Anne and her daughter were well educated, and the pair ran a school after the war. Mary Tucker Magill also wrote several novels and authored a widely used textbook on Virginia history. Jackson, according to Mary Anna, was so found of Mrs. Magill that he "found her a spirit congenial to his own, and so admired her bright and radiant disposition." After one visit, Jackson even told Mary Anna "that when she grew to be an old lady, he hoped she would be 'just like Mrs. Magill.'"

Also living just a few blocks south on Braddock Street from the Grahams were the parents of Jackson's medical director, Dr. Hunter McGuire. His father, Dr. Hugh McGuire, was the founder of the Winchester Medical

Henry Kyd Douglas, youngest member of Stonewall Jackson's staff and the author of *I Rode with Stonewall*. Many historians believe that Douglas's book was written to impress Sallie Conrad, who ended up marrying someone else. *Courtesy of BR/GQ.*

College and one of the most respected physicians in Virginia. The family lived at the corner of Amherst and Braddock Streets. He and his wife, Anna, had eight children, all of them much older than the Grahams' children. Dr. Hunter McGuire was the couple's fifth child; the four oldest were all daughters. His three other sons, Edward, Hugh and William, all served in either the Confederate army or navy during the war.

Hunter's father also served as a surgeon in the Confederate army, and both he and Hunter held the rank of major. The youthful Dr. Hunter McGuire had even more trouble convincing his father of his authority as medical director of Jackson's command than he did convincing Jackson that he was old enough to hold it. During an engagement early in the war, Hunter's father was treating a wounded soldier near the battle line. Concerned, Hunter sent an aide to order his father to a safer place. When the aide approached the elder McGuire and told him of his son's order, he replied sharply, "You tell Hunter to go to hell!"

Besides the McGuires and Magills, the Jacksons made friends with many other Winchester families. The Kent Street Presbyterian Church was also

Kent Street Presbyterian Church. Located at the intersection of Boscawen and Kent Streets, this was where Stonewall Jackson worshiped while he was in Winchester. It is the only site associated with Stonewall Jackson and Winchester that is not standing today. *Courtesy of WFCHS.*

Sallie Conrad, daughter of Robert Y. Conrad and Henry Kyd Douglas's Winchester love interest during the Civil War. *Courtesy of BR/GQ.*

the church home of several families who had soldiers in Jackson's army. The Bell, Holliday and Conrad families all attended Dr. Graham's church, as did a large number of soldiers in Jackson's army who were camped just north of town. Robert Y. Conrad had been friends with Jackson since the early days of the war, and at least one other member of Conrad's family had attracted the attention of one of Jackson's staff officers.

Henry Kyd Douglas, while in Winchester, was probably a regular attendee at Dr. Graham's church since he had taken a fancy to Conrad's pretty daughter, Sallie. The son of a minister, Douglas was, at times, the victim of jealousy among Jackson's staff. Considered by the girls of Winchester to be quite handsome, Douglas usually attracted more attention from them than the other members of the staff. Douglas, however, did not have eyes for anyone in town except Sallie, and at her encouragement, he kept a diary during the war that eventually was published under the title *I Rode with Stonewall*. Unfortunately for the smitten Douglas, Sallie married another.

Mary Anna was favorably impressed with the congregation at the Kent Street Church, particularly the Conrads. She believed "these ladies were conspicuous for their lovely Christian characters—being foremost in all good works, in the hospitals ministering to the soldiers—and wherever they went their lives were devoted to the relief of suffering and to doing good." Of Mrs. Conrad, she said, "Although in the decline of her life, [she] retained much beauty, of brunette style, and in manner was a most gentle and gracious lady." Mary Anna was equally impressed by her two daughters, whom she said "inherited their mother's grace and beauty."

The Grahams, Magills, Conrads and McGuires were not the only families to entertain the Jacksons while they were in Winchester. Wherever the Jacksons went, Mary Anna found "the Winchester ladies were among the most famous of Virginia housekeepers, and live in a great deal of old-fashioned elegance and profusion." After the war, she remembered:

> *The memories of that sojourn in our "war home" are among the most precious and sacred of my whole life. It was there that I was permitted to be the longest time with my husband after he entered the army. He was in such fine health and spirits that, with the exception of the Romney expedition, there was nothing to mar the perfect enjoyment of these blessed three months.*

While living with the Grahams, Jackson kept a tight schedule. "He was strictly methodical," Graham remembered.

> *He invariably rose at a certain hour—which was always early—and went at once to headquarters, where he received his mail, and issued the general orders of the day. A few minutes before 8 o'clock he returned, and always escorted Mrs. Jackson to breakfast, and indeed to every meal. She knew just*

when to expect him, for the clock was not more regular in its movements than was he, and she would wait in her room till he arrived. And in not a single instance I believe, was the meal delayed so much as a minute, by his failure to appear on time.

In general, Graham found Jackson to be "congenial and considerate." Because of the general's status and fame, the Grahams were at times inundated with well-wishers. To all of them, Jackson "had a pleasant word" that was "spoken in a tone that was very gentle, and with an expression of countenance peculiarly winning." One thing Jackson never allowed was for official business to be discussed at the Graham house. If he was required to see a courier or issue a written order, he always left the Graham house and took care of his business at the Moore house, which he still retained as his headquarters and at which he spent much of his day.

The three things the Grahams remember most about their famous houseguest were his "absorbing devotion to his wife," his "fondness for children" and his Christian character. Jackson's tenderness to his wife was something that the Grahams could not help from noticing: "His chivalrous deference to Mrs. Jackson, his unfailing gentleness toward her, his delicate attentions, in which there was never anything of connubial dotage, were something beautiful to see."

He added that Mary Anna was truly worthy of the attention that her husband gave her. He described her as "fair in person, and beautiful in character—amiable and loving in nature—intelligent, cultivated, refined and pious. She possessed all the qualities that could attract the love of this noble man, and lead him to enshrine her in his heart of hearts."

Jackson's fondness for children, however, triggered behavior that would surely have shocked his soldiers camped just north of town, as well as friends who knew him well. On several occasions, Jackson entered one of the Graham rooms while they were entertaining company and got down on all fours with young Alfred, the Grahams' three-year-old son, riding on his back, playing cavalryman. It was an act that Graham jokingly called "shocking," particularly when Alfred would refer to Jackson as "horse."

When several young officers from the Stonewall Brigade came to the Graham house to pay their respects to Mrs. Jackson, they almost immediately went into a room next to where the adults had assembled. When Jackson and the other adults heard a loud, raucous mêlée in the other room, the general went to investigate. What he found was his young officers playing "war" with the Graham children. When he entered, the room fell deathly silent.

Jackson, looking deadly serious, solemnly ordered, "Captain Marye, report this engagement tomorrow—along with the casualties." Jackson smiled, took a seat and watched the conclusion of the battle.

What Graham noticed most was Jackson's Christian character:

> *While eminent in many things, he was pre-eminent for his abiding trust in God. It was not ordinary faith that penetrated his entire being, and held him in complete possession. He was simply a humble, earnest, devout, consecrated Christian man. He was a man of God first and last, and always. He feared God, and tried to serve Him. He believed the Scriptures to be the word of God. Divinely inspired, and therefore infallible.*

Jackson not only attended Kent Street Presbyterian Church on a regular basis while in Winchester but also on occasion visited other denominations. In late February 1862, he attended a prayer meeting at the Christ Episcopal Church. The rector of the church, J.B.T. Reed, asked him to pray. Rising from his seat, Jackson led the congregation in prayer with such fervor that he could be heard easily throughout the church.

According to Kate Sperry, who kept a 650-page diary during the war, while Jackson was leading the congregation at the Loudoun Street Presbyterian Church in prayer, "the church was crowded and by way of enlivening the crowd and the especial edification of said church a young lady, by the name of Josephine Singleton, concluded to have a fit." Sperry, whose diary exposes her as just a little boy crazy, also recorded that Jackson was "right nice looking."

Reverend Benjamin Brooke, pastor of the Market Street Methodist Church, was also in the audience and had this comment: "A woman fainted during the service—all heads were turned to see but Gen. Jackson kept his eyes steadfastly fixed on the altar, nor changed a muscle of his face." Ignoring the outburst, Jackson continued to pray. Brooke added, "I have never witnessed such respect for the house of God. If he fights as he prays—short and to the point—he will apt to do some execution. That prayer indicates a great mind for execution."

Having lived in close quarters with the Jacksons for about six weeks, Graham felt that he knew Jackson's personal habits and character traits as well as anyone and was annoyed by stories that circulated, both during and after the war, about Jackson's peculiarities. When Graham was informed of these peculiarities, he began "to watch for the oddities alleged to him." During Jackson's stay, Graham asserted, "My powers of discernment were not sufficient to detect what was so patent to others." He found that, "whether riding, walking, sitting or conversing, there was nothing in [Jackson's] manner to attract special observation, or to call for remark of any kind."

One thing that particularly upset Graham was the belief by many that Jackson slept through every sermon. Graham admitted that there were times during his sermons when Jackson's looks were "strongly suggesting of a state of somnolency." On one occasion, Graham was preaching on the subject of taking an oath when an enemy army was occupying Winchester. During the sermon, he observed that Jackson seemed sound asleep. Later in the day, when Graham quizzed the general on what he thought of his sermon, "he concisely, but accurately, repeated the substance of the sermon, in which, he declared himself greatly interested because of its timeliness. He had not been asleep."

Jackson shared a physical handicap with another famous American. Like Jackson, Benjamin Franklin was hard of hearing. Franklin, in order to concentrate during the Constitutional Convention, used to close his eyes. Many of the other delegates believed the elderly Franklin was dozing off during the debates and, in fun, would ask him questions to which Franklin would immediately give clear and concise answers. He was not asleep, either.

6

"The Glory Has Departed from Shiloh"

As winter turned to spring in 1862, Jackson's military situation in the northern Shenandoah Valley was not nearly as blissful as his domestic life. His forces, due to the removal of most of Loring's men and the usual number of sick soldiers, had shrunk to about five thousand. Facing him were two Union armies, each of which dwarfed the number of men Jackson could bring to bear. To the north, General Nathaniel Banks commanded an army of around thirty-eight thousand men. To the west lurked another Union army of almost equal size. Johnston, at Manassas, was incapable of sending any reinforcements since he faced the newly named Army of the Potomac, under General George B. McClellan, which outnumbered Johnston's force by about four to one.

As bad as the situation was in Virginia, it was worse elsewhere. After a successful 1861, the Confederacy suffered several disasters to begin 1862 that left many in doubt about whether the new nation could survive the spring. General Ulysses S. Grant, after capturing both Forts Henry and Donelson, had occupied Nashville, Tennessee, and was marching south toward Mississippi. Early in March, the Confederacy also suffered a reverse in the Trans-Mississippi at the Battle of Pea Ridge.

Jackson, despite developments elsewhere and the overwhelming odds against him, was still full of fight. His superior, General Johnston, however, had other plans. Facing an army of over 100,000 men under McClellan, Johnston intended to fall back slowly, covering Richmond in the process. He expected Jackson to withdraw as well, covering the Manassas army's left flank, protecting the Blue Ridge passes and, above all else, keeping

Banks from reinforcing McClellan. Although Jackson's correspondence with Johnston was tactful, he had no intention of quitting Winchester without a fight.

What Jackson could not have known, though, was that McClellan was planning to move his huge army by boat to the Virginia peninsula. Landing at Fort Monroe, he intended to flank Johnston and storm Richmond from the east. Johnston, under those circumstances would be forced to retreat to the peninsula to counter McClellan's move. This left Jackson isolated in the Valley and badly outnumbered. His only possible reinforcements were General Richard Ewell's division east of the Blue Ridge near Madison Court House and General Allegheny Johnson's small force guarding the western approaches to Staunton over one hundred miles to the south. Neither would be of any help if Banks acted quickly.

General Nathaniel Banks, commander of Union forces during the 1862 Shenandoah Valley Campaign and the First Battle of Winchester, May 26, 1862. *Courtesy of BR/GQ.*

It is pure speculation to say that Jackson's reason for not wanting to abandon Winchester was entirely personal. There is, however, a great deal of circumstantial evidence in Jackson's behavior and general philosophy of war to argue that he did not wish to abandon the people of Winchester to a Union occupation without a fight. His opinion about the strategic importance of the Shenandoah Valley was emphatic: "If the Valley is lost, Virginia is lost." His position on offensive warfare was also well known. His personal behavior and the testimony of his wife during the first two weeks of March also lend credence to the view that the defense of Winchester had become very personal.

While Jackson pondered his options, the people of Winchester were well aware of the situation and were in a state of near panic. It was also easy for Jackson's soldiers to understand the odds they faced as Banks inched toward

Kate McVicar, a famed Winchester journalist who wrote under the name "Nemo," was a teenager during the Civil War. Her columns in the *Winchester Times* and the *Evening Star* allowed local citizens to tell their stories about Stonewall Jackson. *Courtesy of THL.*

the Valley town. During this stressful time, one of Winchester's most prolific writers on the town's role in the Civil War met Jackson for the first time. Kate McVicar was a teenage girl who lived north of town on the Valley Turnpike. Her brother and father were both serving in Jackson's army, and from the beginning of the war to her last breath in the twentieth century, McVicar was a rabid Confederate and a great admirer of Jackson.

Living outside of town, though, she had few opportunities to venture into Winchester to see the famous soldier. During the first two weeks of March, however, Jackson spent much of his day north of town studying his position and listening to scouting reports from Ashby's cavalry. Fifty years later, as a writer for the *Evening Star*, McVicar wrote of those days. According to her, on March 11, 1862, "I saw Jackson for the first time. He rode rapidly to the front."

Later, the general "returned more slowly." On his ride back, Jackson gave the young girl the thrill of her life: "I must have looked my youthful enthusiasm for he bowed courteously as he passed and no monarch on earth could have seemed so grand to me. And after all these years I can clearly recall that mild March day, with the sun not far above the western hills and its golden light falling over the hero we loved so well." McVicar voiced the opinion, "There were rumors that Jackson would evacuate the Lower Valley, but no one could or would believe it." She believed that it "would have been rank infidelity to doubt that Jackson was infallible."

At her home in downtown Winchester, Kate Sperry recorded similar feelings: "The people are all crazy—perfectly frantic for fear this place will be evacuated and the Yanks nab them—I don't believe Jackson will leave us without a hard fight which he is to all appearances preparing for." With adulation like that, it is little wonder that Jackson was determined to desperately defend Winchester.

Even people who were not natives of Winchester were terribly upset at the prospect of Jackson's departure. They were not dedicated followers of the Confederacy but had a higher calling. They were colporteurs in Winchester at the invitation of Jackson to hand out Christian tracts to the soldiers. One wrote several months after the evacuation, "Three or four of us were busily engaged in spiritual labors among the soldiers." They were amazed at the

Kate Sperry, a teenage Winchester Civil War diarist who thought that Stonewall Jackson was "right nice looking." *Courtesy of WFCHS.*

response they got from the common soldier in Jackson's ranks: "During my whole stay, only two soldiers refused to take tracts from me—one of whom was unable to read." When they were forced to leave at the approach of Banks's army, one wrote later, "I lay my pen down with sadness, as I remember that Winchester is now in the enemy's possession."

Not all of the people in Winchester, however, were counting on the town's hero to save them from Banks's army. A few were seeing Banks's approach as liberation rather than occupation. To the Unionists in town, Jackson was no hero. Many, including at least two members of the Stonewall Brigade, were sending information to the approaching Union army about Jackson's strength and defensive positions. Lieutenant Arthur Markell of the Fifth Virginia Infantry and Private Jacob Piosel of the Second Virginia Infantry both deserted in early March and provided the Union army facing Winchester with very accurate information about Jackson's army.

Jackson noticed a new aggressiveness in Banks's movements. Civilians in town were also suspected of passing on intelligence to Banks's army. Earlier, Jackson had been reluctant to arrest Unionists in town, but under these new circumstances, his position became much harsher. Feeling that to leave Unionists in Winchester would give Banks even more useful information, he decided to arrest several of the more outspoken ones and send them south. One of those selected for arrest was the father of Unionist diarist Julia Chase.

She recorded in her diary on March 10, "We are expecting nothing else but Father will be arrested, as we learn the secessionists have 150 names down of the Union people." The next day, her worst fears were realized when her father was arrested: "To take an old man lying sick on this sofa is outrageous." She added that the older men "had the privilege of riding to Strasburg by paying a fee. The rest had to walk. Sad, sad day to us." Chase was wrong concerning the number taken. Instead of 150, Jackson only removed about 20 citizens.

For Mrs. Jackson and the Grahams, the evacuation of Winchester was deeply personal. The commencement of hostilities between the two armies would surely bring an end to Mary Anna's sojourn in Winchester. In early March, the situation had become so dangerous that Mary Anna stated, "Early in March, when he found that he would be compelled to retire from Winchester, although his heart was yearning to stay and defend the place, he thought it was no longer safe for me to remain, and I was sent away on the same train which conveyed the sick to a place of safety."

To reach that train, Mary Anna would have to board the stage for Strasburg. Before she left, "He told me that when his 'sunshine' was gone out of the room which had been to us the holy of holies on earth that winter, he never wanted to enter it again." Jackson, although inwardly in great distress over the prospects of the upcoming retreat, "lingered at the door of the coach in which I left with bright smiles, and not a cloud upon his peaceful brow."

Mary Anna described her trip south: "No ray of sunshine lightened the gloom." Perhaps she would not have been so gloomy had she known that her "Winchester Campaign" had proved successful. While she made her journey away from the man she loved, something wonderful was quietly growing inside her.

Jackson's farewell to the Grahams was even more painful. On March 11, Jackson did something that he almost never did: he revealed his military plans to Graham. At dinner that night, Graham commented that it would be unlikely that they would ever see Jackson again. To Graham's surprise, he "was all aglow with pleasant excitement because of the splendid behavior of his troops, and their eagerness to meet the enemy, who had been seen, but who, without offering battle, had gone into camp."

Mrs. Mary Greenhow Lee, Winchester's most prolific diarist, begged Stonewall Jackson not to leave Winchester in the fall of 1862. Her over nine-hundred-page diary was recently edited by Eloise C. Strader, a founding member of the Kernstown Battlefield Association, and was published in 2012 by the Winchester–Frederick County Historical Society. *Courtesy of BR/GQ.*

That evening after a prayer service at Graham's home, the people there were full of gloom over the likely prospect of Jackson's army leaving that night. As tears began to fall among those present, Jackson reassured them, "O, I'll see you again! I am not leaving you." Unknown to those at the Grahams, Jackson was planning a night attack in the hope that a surprise at night would conceal his woefully outnumbered army.

Unfortunately, later that night, when Jackson held a council of war with his top commanders at the Moore house, his plan for a night attack was looked upon with horror, and all urged an immediate withdrawal. They also informed him that the supply wagons, which were supposed to be parked just south of town, had actually traveled all the way to Newtown. His soldiers had also marched that distance and would have to march back the twelve miles from Newtown before the attack could be launched. Jackson's cheery mood changed to anger, but there was now no choice; he had to evacuate Winchester.

Before he left, though, he had to return to his friend and host and give him the bad news. When Jackson arrived, Graham stated, "he was bitterly distressed and mortified at the necessity of leaving the people he loved dearly." Even at that late hour, Jackson was still not convinced that the night attack was impossible. "He paced the room a minute or two in painful indecision, then suddenly passing before me, with his hand grasping the hilt of his sword as if he would crush it, and his face blazing with the fire that was burning in his soul, he said, 'I may execute my purpose still.'"

That, however, was a forlorn hope, and after meeting again at the Moore house with a few of his officers, he ordered the evacuation. Outside his headquarters, he approached Graham "with an air of intense grief [and] proposed to return with me and take leave of my family." During his last statement to the Graham family before he left Winchester, "he had recovered his composure, tho' not his cheerfulness, and expressing the hope that a good Providence would permit him to soon return, and bring deliverance to the town, he bade us a touching farewell."

Jackson rode out of town with another Winchester resident he had grown to admire. While riding with Dr. Hunter McGuire, the young doctor began to weep quietly as they headed south together. Turning to look at Jackson, McGuire saw that the general's face "was fairly blazing with the fire that was burning in him." Jackson's facial expression bore the marks of a bitterly disappointed man. His muscles twitched, and his lips were tightly compressed. Looking back at Winchester as they rode past the city limits, he loudly remarked, "That is the last council of war I will ever hold!"

The morning of March 12, 1862, was a day that no one who lived in Winchester would ever forget. The citizens reeled in shock as the troops of General Banks's army entered the town to the tune of "John Brown's Body." The Union army could not have picked a more divisive melody to play since the Brown Raid had occurred just twenty short miles from the town. It was remembered by everyone that Brown's plan had included the genocide of all white Southerners in the name of setting up a Negro Republic. It was also vividly remembered that the first person killed in Brown's Raid was a free black man named Heyward Shepherd, a resident of Winchester.

Several women of Winchester had started keeping diaries over the past year, but the one that would be the longest and most thorough was begun on the day of the first Union occupation. Mrs. Mary Greenhow Lee lived on Cameron Street next door to the Bartons. Unlike most Winchester residents, she grew up east of the Blue Ridge, could trace her ancestry back to the earliest settlers in the colony and was a true Virginia blueblood. Surprisingly, she had not yet met Jackson, although she was a great admirer.

Mrs. Lee took a more sober approach to the arrival of the Union army and was glad Jackson had not attempted to defend the town, "as it will do no good, in the end, & will only draw on us poor helpless ones the fury of a defeated army or the additional insolence of a victorious one." As the Union soldiers entered town, her objectivity seemed to wane: "All is over & we are prisoners in our own homes. For about an hour, a death like stillness pervaded the town, & then music & some cheering announced their approach."

Her next-door neighbor, Major Frank Jones's sister Fanny Barton, "was standing on her porch when some passed & she went & slammed her door & locked it & one of them said 'there is a d__ secessionist'." Feelings were running just as high on Loudoun Street. Kate Sperry recorded, "It must be told—'the glory has departed from Shiloh.' To think that all of our trouble in fortifying the town for the enemy to come and take quiet possession is too much."

The one Confederate who gained in reputation by the departure of Jackson's army was Colonel Turner Ashby. The last Confederate soldier to leave Winchester, his story, whether true or not, was certainly believed by the admiring young ladies of town. There are several versions. Sperry told it this way in her diary:

> *Col. Ashby didn't leave here until about 15 minutes before the main body of the enemy came in—he was riding slowly out of town and happened to see one of the yanks, who had come in advance of the rest—the first one, about,*

> *that had come, Ashby jumped off his horse, collared the fellow, demanded his arms and made him get* *<u>up behind</u>* *him and rode off at a round rate with his prisoner.*

Whether the story is true, its telling reveals that although Jackson's army was gone, the town was in no mood to surrender. Years later, Kate McVicar would remark in her newspaper column that Banks's occupation was the mildest of the many that Winchester endured during the war. The defiance of the women in town during this period, however, gave Winchester a reputation that has endured through the years—that of fierce resistance to the Union armies in the Valley but also an almost tireless mercy to the sick and wounded of their hated enemy. Whether Union or Confederate, it would be the most trying time in the history of the town, but it would also be remembered, for the citizens and their favorite general, as their finest hour.

7
"Winchester Is a Very Pleasant Place to Stay In, Sir"

The soldiers marching with Jackson south to Strasburg had equally strong opinions about the evacuation of Winchester. But unlike the citizens in town, these men were hardened veterans. Disappointment was intense over leaving their families and friends in the hands of the enemy, but it was also balanced with hard military logic. A battle at Winchester would have been, at best, a bloody encounter and probably would have resulted in the town being evacuated anyway. At worst, a defeat might have destroyed their army, leaving the Valley permanently in the hands of the Union army.

With Colonel James Allen and Lieutenant Colonel Lawson Botts absent from the Second Virginia Infantry at the time of its withdrawal, Major Frank Jones led the regiment south with the rest of Jackson's army. "We marched out with heavy hearts & bivouacked on the turnpike four miles from Winchester." Jones did not write this passage in a letter to his wife or mother. Just before leaving Winchester, his wife, Susan, gave him a small notebook and urged him to keep a diary. His comments about the march south from Winchester were his first entry in a diary that chronicled one of the most dramatic events of the war: Jackson's Valley Campaign.

Another Winchester native who was marching with Jackson had received an important promotion. Private Hugh Barr was well known to the soldiers heading south. As a teenager, he had marched up and down the streets of Winchester, beating the rally on his drum, "calling Virginians to arms to repel the threatened invasion of John Brown." Enlisting in Captain Stover Funk's Marion Rifles at the beginning of the war, his ability with a drum was noticed, and just before the withdrawal, Barr was transferred to the staff of the Fifth Virginia Infantry as regimental drum major.

There were several other Winchester soldiers marching either with Jones and his regiment or with some other unit within the Stonewall Brigade. At least one of them was a new recruit. Robert Barton, who had enlisted in the Second Virginia Infantry early in the war only to be rejected due to poor health, had enlisted in the Rockbridge Artillery on March 7. There, he joined his brother David, who was also with the battery.

His attempt to get back into the war was, at first, unsuccessful. In his memoirs, Barton lamented, "We march on and marched back again, through wind and rain, cold snow and wet, without tents or other protection, sleeping on the wet ground in wet clothes and eating such food as we could get and eat, which was bad enough." It did not take long before "this life drove me to the hospital and I was carried back to Staunton." By the time Robert got back to his battery, another new recruit had joined. On March 28, Private Robert E. Lee Jr., the youngest son of the general, reported for duty with the Rockbridge Artillery. He, along with Robert Mims from

The Magill house on North Loudoun Street, home of Ann Tucker and Mary Tucker Magill during the Civil War. General James Shields stayed at this house during the early phases of the 1862 Shenandoah Valley Campaign. The house has had many alterations since the war. *Courtesy of WFCHS.*

Baltimore, Maryland, became fast friends with the sickly Barton. Together, they were known in the battery as the "Three Bobs."

Jackson stayed at Strasburg two days before marching his army south to Rude's Hill, just a few miles south of Mount Jackson. As he marched south, the civilians in the area were as disheartened as the people of Winchester to see his army leave them. The march, however, was leisurely, and his soldiers arrived at Rude's Hill in good spirits. New recruits, like Robert Barton and others returning from leave, swelled his ranks, but not enough for him to challenge Banks.

General James Shields's Union division of Banks's command followed Jackson as far as Strasburg. Ashby's cavalry covered the withdrawal with such efficiency that Shields was unable to get much information on Jackson's strength or whereabouts. None of that mattered, though. General McClellan's Army of the Potomac was moving his army to the Virginia peninsula for its march on Richmond and did not believe that Jackson's 4,600-man army was much of a threat to Washington. Less than a week after Banks occupied Winchester, McClellan ordered him to move most of his army to Manassas to cover Washington while he was away.

When Ashby reported that the Union army in the Valley was preparing to move east, Jackson immediately ordered a pursuit. His orders from General Johnston required him not to allow any Union forces to leave the Valley to reinforce McClellan. As Shields withdrew north, Ashby's cavalry, supported by Captain Roger Preston Chew's Horse Artillery, stayed close on his heels. All of this seemed to bring an opportunity not only to obey Johnston's orders but to return to Winchester as well.

While the two forces were jockeying for position, the people of Winchester were anything but passive toward the Union soldiers in town. Shields, who decided to make his headquarters at the home of the famed hostess Anne Tucker Magill, got an unforgettable reception from her daughter. Over supper one evening, she looked the general in the face and blurted out that if the Federals killed "all the men of the South, the women would fight, and that when they were all destroyed the dogs would bark at them."

The Magills were more gracious than most though. Peyton Clark, Frank Jones's brother-in-law, refused Union officers any accommodations, as did the Conrads. When a large Union flag was hosted on Loudoun Street, the women refused to walk underneath it. When it was removed and replaced by one hanging completely over the street, the women walked in the gutter rather than beneath it. Although most Confederate sympathizers in town admitted later that Banks's occupation was mild in comparison to others, the situation in Winchester was tense.

General James Shield. Although he was not on the battlefield that day, he was the overall Union commander at the First Battle of Kernstown, March 23, 1862. *Courtesy of BR/GQ.*

With information about these incidents surely leaking back to Jackson and his army, the desire to retake Winchester must have been fierce among the general and his army. With word that Banks was leaving the Valley, Jackson left Rude's Hill early on March 22, heading north toward Winchester. It was the first of a series of forced marches over the next two and a half months that would earn his command the nickname "Jackson's Foot Cavalry."

Although the men were in high spirits, the grueling twenty-five-mile march left many on the roadside from exhaustion. After camping near Strasburg that evening, his army arrived just south of Kernstown about 2:00 p.m. on Sunday, March 23. Having covered nearly thirty-five miles in two days, stragglers had reduced Jackson's total force to less than 3,500 men of all arms when it arrived at the small hamlet just five miles south of Winchester. It was also the Sabbath, and the earnest Presbyterian had strong reservations about disturbing the Lord's Day.

While Jackson's men were tramping north to Kernstown, Ashby was fighting a seesaw battle with Union forces along the Valley Turnpike south of Winchester. Heavily outnumbered, Ashby's men were unable to ascertain the true Union strength facing them. He reported to Jackson that there were only four Union regiments and a couple of batteries in his front. The actual strength was over four times that number. Ashby did extract a little revenge for Jackson's friends, the Magills. A shot from Chew's Battery painfully broke Shields's arm and forced him from the field on the twenty-second.

The ground directly in front of the Confederate position was not inviting, though. Pritchard's Hill, on the west side of the Valley Pike just north of Kernstown, dominated all of the area to the south and east. Just a mile and a half to the west of Pritchard's Hill, however, was Sandy Ridge. Taking Sandy Ridge would flank Pritchard's Hill and open the way to Winchester.

The Union forces guarding Pritchard's Hill also had a clear view south and could easily see what they were up against. Although Jackson believed that the force in front of him was small, it was impossible to know how many additional Union forces were close enough to provide reinforcements. If he waited until Monday, the enemy might withdraw, and he would miss an opportunity to crush them. If reinforcements were close enough, he might lose the opportunity to retake Winchester. Jackson understood that if he were going to confront the Union forces in front of him, he needed to do it immediately. Despite the Sabbath, he could not ignore the opportunity and decided to attack.

To his soldiers, who had already been in several battles with Jackson, his mannerism when serious fighting was about to take place was familiar. His facial muscles had a tendency to twitch when on a battlefield. This was so pronounced that one soldier in his command jokingly referred to it as "Old Jack making faces at the Yankees."

Although the sun was beginning to set on the western horizon before Jackson had everything ready, he ordered four regiments of the Stonewall Brigade, the Twenty-third and Thirty-seventh Virginia under Colonel Sam Fulkerson, with Carpenter's Battery in support, to take Sandy Ridge. The Fifth Virginia Infantry was held in reserve since nearly one hundred men were without weapons. The rest of the forces under Jackson would remain near Pritchard's Hill to occupy the Union forces there. It was about 4:00 p.m.

One key advantage that Jackson had was Major Frank Jones. His farm, Carysbrook, was only a short distance from Pritchard's Hill, and he was intimately familiar with the terrain. During the battle, he served as a courier for Jackson, as well as explaining to him the lay of the land.

The dominant feature on Sandy Ridge was a stone wall located on its northern end. While Jackson was attempting to flank the Union position

Hugh Barr, a Winchester native, was originally a member of the Marion Rifles, Company A, Fifth Virginia Infantry, but was transferred to the staff of the Stonewall Brigade in early 1862. He was the drummer boy whom Stonewall Jackson ordered to beat the rally during the final stages of the First Battle of Kernstown. *Courtesy of BR/GQ.*

by taking Sandy Ridge, a Union brigade under Colonel Erastus Tyler was attempting to do the same thing to the Confederates. Colonel James Allen remarked, "On arriving in the wood I occupied a sheltered position with my command and went across the ridge to report to General R.B. Garnett." Ahead of Allen was the stone wall. "Major [Frank] Jones again ordered us forward."

Allen, along with the rest of the Stonewall Brigade, raced frantically to reach the stone wall before Tyler's brigade. Jackson's men won and released a brutal volley at point-blank range. Reeling from the volley, Tyler's men still remained near the stone wall, and a vicious fight erupted between the two forces. Colonel Arthur Cummings, commanding the Thirty-third Virginia Infantry, described the fighting along the stone wall: "We kept up an incessant fire upon the enemy for about one and a half hours, who were pressing upon us in largely superior numbers and pouring into our ranks a deadly fire."

Jones, who was near the fighting at the stone wall recalled in his diary, "The most terrific fire of musketry that can be imagined commenced and continued for one hour and 35 minutes, until nearly dark." The Winchester Major wrote almost nothing about his part in the battle, but he was mentioned in almost every Confederate official report of the day's fighting. Allen stated, "Major Jones I observed frequently during the day in the most exposed positions in discharge of his duties to the major-general."

The Stonewall Brigade, under General Richard Garnett, held the center of the line on Sandy Ridge. Fulkerson's two-regiment brigade was on his right flank, and another small brigade under Colonel Jesse Burk was on Garnett's left. As the fighting intensified, Jackson began to realize that he was facing a much larger force than he expected. He sent his young staff officer, Sandie Pendleton, to ascertain the situation. When Pendleton returned, he gave Jackson the first accurate information on the true strength of the Union forces opposing them. Jackson's response was, "Say nothing about it, but we are in for it."

Participants from both sides called the fighting at the stone wall on Sandy Ridge as violent as any they experienced during the war. Even considering that many of the Union soldiers were in their first battle, their comments on the carnage left no doubt that the fighting there was terrific. One Union veteran of the battle stated, "The infantry fire, to the extent of the line, was as heavy as it was at Antietam, Gettysburg, or the Wilderness."

The battle did not go unnoticed by the people of Winchester, who could clearly hear from their homes the massive concussions of artillery and musket fire. They could also witness Union soldiers moving quickly through town toward the battlefield. Kate Sperry recorded in her diary that day, "More and more men are being sent out this afternoon. We could hear the cannon distinctly, boom! boom!"

Peyton Clark recorded in his journal:

> *Service was conducted in the Presbyterian Churches as usual by their respective ministers. After service the discharges became more frequent and nearer until about three o'clock they seemed to be within three miles of the town and the roar of musketry, which was now distinct, and cannon became incessant. The suspense was terrible and anxiety and distress marked every countenance.*

Mrs. Lee, from her home on Cameron Street, stated, "In a little while I heard great excitement in the streets, & the firing of cannon and musketry

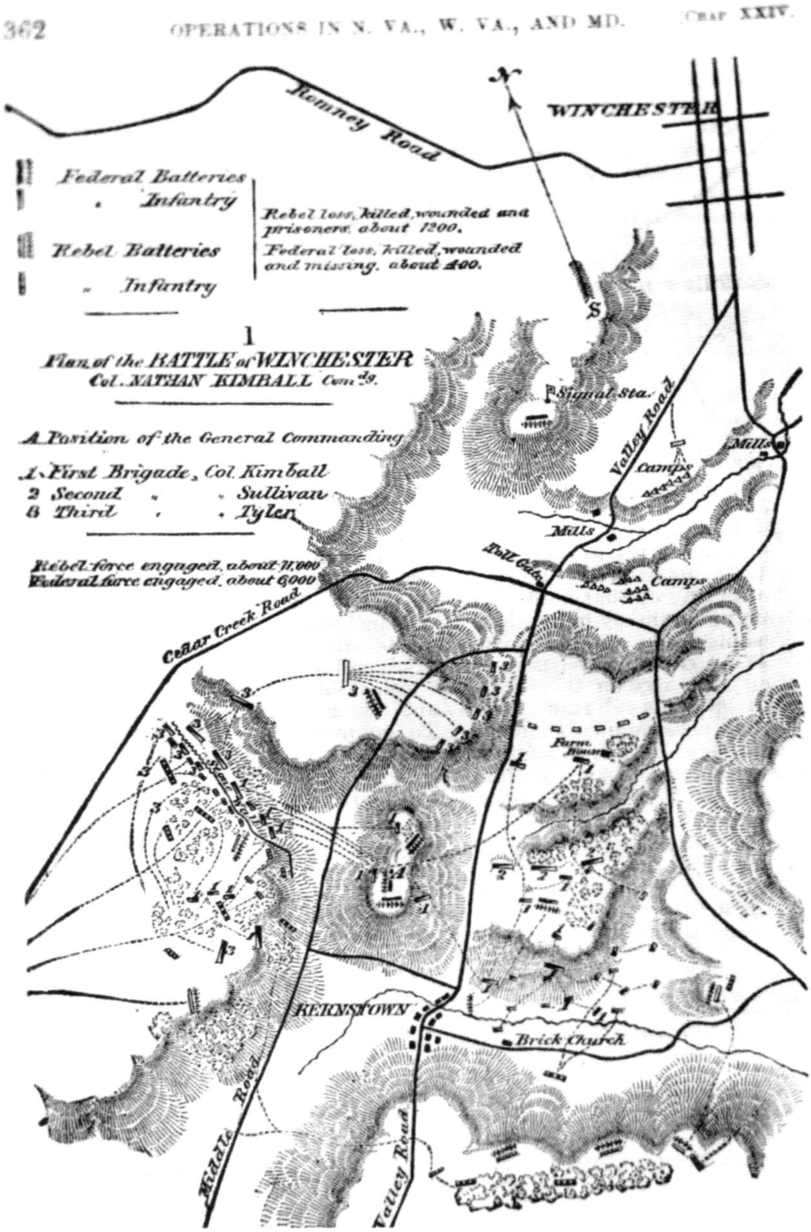

Map of the First Battle of Kernstown, March 23, 1862. *Courtesy of WFCHS.*

was very near." It seems that many of the people in town were trying to get ringside seats to watch the battle. "First Mrs. Barton came in, she had been on top of Mrs. [Anne Tucker] Magill's house, where she could see the fight. We stood on the porch, we could hear the guns every minute. Cornelia and I ran up to Mr. [Robert Y.] Conrad's, & joined the girls on top of their house."

If there was any doubt how the majority of people in Winchester felt about the battle, a story told by Kate McVicar made it clear:

> *A Federal officer was boarding with a family north of Winchester. The father of the family and a son were with Jackson. On the day of the battle of Kernstown, the officer asked the daughter of the family, a bright young girl, what wish she would make for him ere he went to fight against her friends, and she said. "I wish you no harm as long as you do no harm to the Southern boys, but the moment that you hurt one of them I wish that the next ball that is fired will go through your heart."*

It is interesting to note that McVicar did not indentify the "bright young girl," but the future journalist did have both a father and a brother fighting with Jackson that day.

With Shields in Winchester recovering from his broken arm, command of the Union forces facing Jackson fell to Colonel Nathan Kimball. Feeding forces from Pritchard Hill to Sandy Ridge, Kimball was putting enormous pressure on the right of Garnett's line. After over an hour and a half of intense fighting, he, Burk and Fulkerson's men were running low on ammunition and in serious danger of being overwhelmed by the much larger Union force. Jackson hoped to hold on until darkness allowed him to withdraw his army quietly. That, however, depended on Garnett's ability to hold Sandy Ridge until nightfall.

Garnett, with Burk and Fulkerson, were facing three Union brigades. Out of ammunition, and the situation growing more desperate by the second, Garnett, without consulting Jackson, made the decision to pull back at about 6:00 p.m. Jackson, who had moved closer to the Confederate position, noticed that the line on Sandy Ridge was crumbling. Fuming with rage, Jackson rode through the retreating Confederates, trying desperately to rally them. Approaching Hugh Barr, Jackson ordered the drummer to beat the "Rally." Terrified, Barr complied, while fleeing Confederate soldiers ran by him in a state of panic and bullets zipped by his head.

Jackson still had two small regiments that could be put into the fight. The Fifth and Forty-second Virginia were still unengaged, and Jackson ordered

The famous stone wall from the First Battle of Kernstown as it looked several years after the battle. The stone wall, which still exists today, is now part of the Rose Hill Farm and is owned by the Museum of the Shenandoah Valley. It is opened to the public once a month for visitors. *Courtesy of WFCHS.*

them to the front. Garnett, however, had already placed the two regiments in defensive positions to cover his retreat. With no troops now available to retake the stone wall, Jackson was left with no choice but to withdraw his small army. The retreat quickly turned into a disorderly rout as the Confederates left their dead and wounded on the field. The disorganized flight finally stopped about three miles from the battlefield, near Bartonsville.

Jackson rode sullenly through the mob south on the Valley Turnpike, stopping at a campfire near the road. There, he stood silently contemplating what had happened. In a battle that lasted a little over three hours, he had lost a fourth of his command. Out of the darkness, one of Ashby's cavalrymen rode up. Seeing Jackson, he commented, "The Yankees don't seem willing to quit Winchester, General." Jackson paused and then barked, "Winchester is a very pleasant place to stay in, sir." Seeing the burning intensity in the general's face, the cavalryman made a quick retreat.

8

"God Blessed Our Arms with Victory at McDowell Yesterday"

While Jackson led his badly beaten army south along the Valley Turnpike, General Shields, who had not witnessed the battle, sent a glowing report to his superiors. Stating that the three-hour battle had lasted eight hours and estimating Jackson's small force to be twice its actual strength, the Union general inadvertently turned Jackson's defeat into a strategic victory. Ordered to prevent the Union army in the Valley from reinforcing McClellan in front of Richmond, the wild exaggeration of Jackson's strength caused officials in Washington to recall Banks's entire army to the Valley.

Although he had lost a fourth of his men during the engagement, Jackson's ranks began to swell as broken-down soldiers who had fallen out on the way to Kernstown returned to their regiments. Although Jackson had told the nosy cavalryman on the road after the battle that he was "satisfied," it was hardly the truth. One of his first acts after the battle was to relieve General Garnett from command of the Stonewall Brigade for withdrawing it from the stone wall without orders. Although the controversy was never resolved to either's satisfaction, Garnett's command of the Stonewall Brigade was over.

The dismissal did not sit well with the members of the brigade. Garnett had been very good at seeing to the comfort of his men, and most of the brigade agreed with his decision to withdraw from Sandy Ridge. Major Frank Jones wrote to his wife, Susan, "Our brigade is astounded at the order & had it not been that the cause was too sacred to jeopardize there would have been considerable commotion made amongst us."

The Frederick County Civil War Courthouse is a Civil War museum today. The area in front the building was used to keep Confederate prisoners, including several from Winchester, after the First Battle of Kernstown. *Courtesy of WFCHS.*

Another reason for the disapproval of the brigade was that, for the second time, Jackson bypassed all the regimental commanders and chose an outsider as Garnett's replacement. General Sidney Winder, who took over the command of the brigade, was a professional soldier and a West Point graduate. He was also a personal friend of Garnett, and the appointment was personally painful for him. When Winder arrived at the brigade camp to take command, the men hissed at him, and the regimental officers would only report to brigade headquarters when ordered to. It was a stormy beginning that would take time to cool down.

Major Frank Jones spent the evening after the battle at his mother's home, Vaucluse, just south of the battlefield. Obviously depressed with the defeat, he recorded in his diary on March 24, "Took leave this morning of my dear mother and looked perhaps for the last time on the sweet envisions of my beloved home." To his wife a few days later, he wrote, "I hope this may reach you. A letter has been recd. this morning from Mrs. Lee & from Mrs. Magill stating our loss of prisoners was 160. I trust it is not so large. We have a number missing but they are coming in. I hope the Yankees don't think there is any panic amongst our troops."

Jones also gave Susan a picture of what Jackson was thinking: "Gen. Jackson is determined to fight those following [us] as soon as possible. We have a large number of noble fellows turning out & the spirit of the people is far better." Jackson agreed. Writing to Mary Anna on the day after the battle, he admitted, "Our men fought bravely, but the superior numbers of the enemy repulsed me." Five days after the battle, though, he wrote to her, "My little army is in excellent spirits. It feels that it inflicted a severe blow upon the enemy."

After passing Woodstock, Jackson paused near Narrow Passage and called on an acquaintance of his from before the war to come to his headquarters. Jedediah Hotchkiss, the principal of a private school near Staunton, was a native of New York. A deeply religious man, Hotchkiss had almost certainly met Jackson before the war when he visited the general's in-laws from his first marriage while on a trip to Lexington. Hotchkiss, just before the beginning of Jackson's march north to Kernstown, had joined the army with about five hundred militiamen from his native Augusta County.

The call of Hotchkiss to Jackson's headquarters was a sure indication of how the general was thinking, even after the defeat at Kernstown. An amateur cartographer, Hotchkiss had a skill that was much needed by Jackson. Upon his arrival at headquarters, Jackson curtly ordered, "I want you to make me a map of the Valley, from Harpers Ferry to Lexington, showing all the points of offense and defense in those places. Mr. [Sandie] Pendleton will give you orders for whatever outfit you want. Good morning, sir."

While Jackson's army was retreating south, the people of Winchester were suddenly learning what it meant to have a battle fought nearby. The casualties began to arrive late on the day of the battle. Only Union soldiers were brought into town initially, leaving the Confederate wounded lying on the battlefield. Public buildings, schools, churches and private homes were quickly transformed into hospitals, and the women and children in town were just as quickly transformed into nurses and hospital orderlies.

A week after the battle, a correspondent for the *Philadelphia Inquirer* reported on the Union wounded: "At the present time there are in three different hospitals, in this town about three hundred wounded soldiers. Fifty have been taken away to their homes in the Northern states by friends." After reporting that the Union Hotel in Winchester had been turned into a hospital, the articles added, "A visit to this hospital is a thing to be remembered. In many of the rooms men are stretched out, suffering from frightful wounds; here a leg has been amputated; the patient, is looking about him in an expression of semi-consciousness."

Two days after the battle, Kate Sperry went to the Union Hotel to visit a Captain Noonan. She wrote, "Poor fellow—he had boarded there for six

The Robert Y. Conrad home at the northeast corner of Boscawen and Cameron Streets. It was torn down in the late twentieth century and is today the site of the Frederick County Courthouse. *Courtesy of BR/GQ.*

months—was a Marylander—so handsome—was shot in the leg—had it amputated yesterday and died this morning at 7 o'clock." The soldier Sperry was referring to was Lieutenant Robert C. Noonan of Frederick County, Maryland. He was serving with the Twenty-first Virginia Infantry when he was wounded.

After commenting that one of the young girls in town thought of Noonan as a brother, Sperry noted that "he was laid out elegantly in a very nice coffin bound with silver—his cap and sword on. I never felt as sad in my life as when I looked at him—he's not more that 22 or 23 at the farthest." Mrs. Lee had also visited Noonan and found, "his wound having received no attention...Dr. Conrad & Dr. Holliday to visit him."

On the day after the battle, Peyton Clark wrote in his journal:

> *The ambulances have been running all day to the battle-field bringing in the wounded. The Court House, York House, Union Hotel, Rouss' Store and house, and other houses are filled, presenting every variety of wound, some of them shocking and distressing to the last degree.*

He went on to add bitterly that local citizens were not allowed to visit the battlefield or the hospitals to see or care for their loved ones. He suspected that the real reason for the refusals was to conceal "the large number of men killed on their side."

As Mrs. Lee had related to Jones, there were large numbers of Confederate prisoners brought to town from the battlefield. Two days after the battle, she found "Sergeant Major [Randolph] Barton, amongst the prisoners." Barton was able to relay to Mrs. Lee the fate of several other local soldiers. "Bob [Robert S. Burwell], Willie [Barton] & Bob Bell were safe, well, & at the jail; it was joyous news." She determined that the next thing to do was "collect a breakfast and take it to them." One of the ironies of the whole situation was that the Barton boys were taken prisoner in, of all places, "Barton Woods," on their family farm.

Despite the horrors of the battlefield, the mounting casualties and the defeat of Jackson, the people of Winchester remained defiant. Clark wrote in his journal:

> *The prisoners were greeted by the ladies of the town with much feeling and boldness from their front doors and porches as they passed up Market* [Cameron] *Street to the depot for transportation north. One of them in my hearing cried out, "Well, Rebels! Remember that Washington was a rebel in his day."*

According to Clark, the response from the Confederate prisoners was, "We fought for you ladies and will be back soon to fight for you again."

A week after the battle, Fanny Graham wrote to Mary Anna Jackson about the battle, conditions in Winchester and the great hope the town had: "Indeed, our old town has stood up bravely for the South—No one succumbs to them or has any thing to do with them." Of the captured Confederate soldiers who passed through town, she stated, "Their greatest happiness seems to consist in the hope to fight for our independence." On General Jackson, she wrote that his soldiers have "the greatest admiration for the General and are crazy to fight under him again."

However, there was another hope that appeared in almost every paragraph of the letter: "I feel quite proud of our town. The [Union] officers threatened to arrest every secessionist, but we are not intimidated & I hope the General will come back before they have time." After signing the letter, Fanny added in postscript, "Give our love to your dear husband—tell him our daily prayer is that his 'head may be covered in the day of battle' & that his efforts may be crowned with success."

Jed Hotchkiss, a native of New York and a distant relative of Harriet Beecher Stowe. He was Stonewall Jackson's mapmaker during the war. *Courtesy of THL.*

Despite the bravado, Jackson's army was still in retreat and reached its old campground at Rude's Hill on April 1, 1862. Banks, who had returned to the Valley after the Battle of Kernstown, pursued Jackson at a leisurely pace, averaging about two miles per day. Staying at Rude's Hill for two weeks, Jackson took advantage of the time to drill his men as his army grew to six thousand thanks to the new conscription act that had been passed. Jackson also had learned of his wife's pregnancy and wrote a short letter to her while she was staying with relatives at Hampden-Sydney College.

A new strategic situation existed as Jackson retreated south. Winchester was the key to offensive operations against vital Union supply links along the Potomac River, but Staunton, Virginia, 130 miles south, was vital to Confederate hopes of defending Richmond. The Valley town was connected to Richmond through the Virginia Central Railroad, and valuable supplies from the Shenandoah Valley traveled through the town to the Confederate capital. If Banks or Fremont were to capture Staunton, it would be a terrible blow to the Confederate army defending Richmond.

On April 18, the army began moving south toward Harrisonburg. Turning east there, the army encamped near Swift Run Gap at the base of the Blue Ridge Mountains. It was a perfect location for an outnumbered army and offered several options. Perhaps the most important one was that it left the impression on Banks that Jackson was in wild retreat and had left the Valley entirely. Messages between the Union Valley commander and General McClellan reveal that this is exactly what he believed. General Shields confirmed that opinion when he wrote to the War Department that Jackson was "flying from the department."

Jackson, however, was only thinking of the offensive and how he could strike and cripple his Union opponents. At Swift Run Gap, hidden from Banks's view, he was in a position to pounce on his rear and left flank if he ventured too close to Staunton. The position also brought Jackson close to General Richard Ewell's eight-thousand-man division near Madison Court House on the east side of the Blue Ridge. Finally, and enticingly, Swift Run Gap put Jackson within supporting distance of General Allegheny Johnson's three-thousand-man division, which was protecting the approaches to Staunton west of the town from General John C. Fremont's army. A concentration of those three commands would raise the number of Jackson's soldiers to twenty thousand men, more than enough to destroy Banks and retake Winchester.

To his subordinates, Jackson, who had kept his promise never to hold another council of war, revealed nothing, and no one had any idea what he was thinking. Many of his men had no idea where they were. Jackson's secretive behavior proved a major irritation to his men and his subordinates, but it probably made possible the maneuver he was planning at Rude's Hill and Swift Run Gap. He did, however, slip once, if ever so slightly, in a letter to a Winchester lady: "I hope that our God in his providence will soon permit me to return to your town of which I have so many pleasant recollections, and see it again under that government which it has shown so much loyalty."

One person who was eyeing Jackson's whereabouts and contemplating how to use his small army was President Jefferson Davis's military advisor, General Robert E. Lee. With Johnston busy watching McClellan inch closer to Richmond every day, Lee took over the task of managing the rest of the Confederate forces in Virginia. His biggest and most dangerous problem was a Union corps, commanded by General Irvin McDowell, which was hovering north of Richmond near Fredericksburg. If it moved south, it would bring a large Union force, not just from the east, but from the north as well, upon Richmond. If that occurred, it might prove fatal to Richmond and the Confederacy. Lee saw a reinforced Jackson, moving north toward Winchester and the vital Union supply links near the Potomac River, as the best chance of keeping McDowell away from Richmond.

Unlike Johnston, Lee did not give Jackson detailed instructions on how to conduct operations in the Shenandoah Valley. What he did do was put General Ewell's eight-thousand-man division under Jackson's control, as well as General Johnson's small command west of Staunton. Concentrated, this gave Jackson the troops he needed to confront Banks on equal terms. Lee's only direct order to Jackson proved to be the perfect one, considering the situation, and became one of the most famous orders of the war. He told Jackson, "The blow wherever struck, must, to be successful, be sudden and heavy."

Ewell's division reached the summit of Swift Run Gap on April 29. Descending the Blue Ridge, most of his men were looking forward to getting their first look at the famous "Stonewall" and his remarkable soldiers. They were in for a disappointment. While Ewell's division filed into camp near Swift Run Gap, to their amazement, Jackson and his entire command had vanished. It looked to Ewell's soldiers as if Jackson had abandoned them. Ewell, who knew more than his men after a meeting with Jackson the day before, still had no idea where Jackson was going. Jackson did not consult any of his subordinate commanders about his plans or movements, and Ewell was completely in the dark.

As May 1862 began and Ewell stewed at Swift Run Gap, the Confederacy had reached its lowest point of the war. In the west, less than three weeks before, a major battle had been fought near a small church called Shiloh. The forty-eight-hour battle there resulted in more than twice the American casualties of the entire Revolutionary War. That had sent shock waves through both the North and South. It had also resulted in a decisive Confederate defeat that left Tennessee almost entirely in Union hands and had opened the way for the occupation of Mississippi. As Jackson's men marched out of Swift Run Gap, New Orleans, the largest port in the South, fell to a combined Federal naval and army force.

In Virginia, the situation was equally dire. As McClellan's army inched almost irresistibly toward Richmond, another Union corps was preparing to pounce on the Confederate capital from the north. In the Shenandoah Valley, Banks threatened the vital rail link at Staunton from the north while an equally large Union army under General John C. Fremont slowly moved toward the Valley town from the west. All that stood between Fremont's twenty-thousand-man army and Staunton was the small, three-thousand-man force under General Allegheny Johnson. To make matters worse for Ewell, his commanding officer had taken six thousand badly needed troops and disappeared.

Most believed, even in Richmond, that the Confederacy was dying, and complete collapse seemed only days away. In the middle of this doom and gloom, on the afternoon of May 9, 1862, a message arrived at the Confederate War Department. The note's origin was from a small hamlet deep within the Appalachian Mountains about twenty-five miles west of Staunton. It was delivered to Adjutant General Samuel Cooper. It read simply, "God blessed our army with victory at McDowell yesterday." It was from Jackson.

9

May 25, 1862

What Jackson had done was march his men from Swift Run Gap southeast through Brown Gap to Meacham Station on the Virginia Central Railroad just west of Charlottesville. Giving the impression that he was headed toward Richmond, he abruptly turned west, traveling by rail to Staunton. From there, he quickly moved west to unite with General Allegheny Johnson's small command. The combined force continued west, searching for General John C. Fremont's Union army.

Arriving just east of the tiny hamlet of McDowell and finding a Union force there, Johnson, who commanded the advance, took position on Sitlington's Hill, east of town. On May 8, he was attacked by the enemy forces in McDowell. A short, bloody battle resulted in a Union repulse. Jackson pursued them until he reached Franklin, a few miles north of McDowell. Satisfied that the timid Fremont was no longer a threat to Staunton, on May 13, he began retracing his steps to the Valley town. His objective was to unite with Ewell's division, pursue and defeat General Nathaniel Banks's army and, for many personal as well as military reasons, liberate Winchester.

The march back to the Shenandoah Valley proved to be difficult. Marching sixty-seven miles from Franklin, deep in the Appalachian Mountains, to Bridgewater just a few miles south of Harrisonburg was grueling, and much of the trek was made during a driving rainstorm. Robert Barton, who had rejoined the Rockbridge Artillery just before the Battle of McDowell, remembered,

May 25, 1862

The rapid and continuous march of the army through the mountainous country west and northwest of Staunton, before and after the battle of McDowell…all the time without tents and many days and night in the cold rain without any sort of shelter except our blankets and oil clothes: separated frequently from the wagon trains and eating raw our fat bacon, at last brought our division back to Harrisonburg.

Major Frank Jones's diary speaks volumes about the arduous marching and fighting of his regiment during this period, not by what he recorded, but by what he left out. After making an entry into his diary every day since the evacuation of Winchester on March 12, he recorded on May 18, "Beautiful morning, lovely Sabbath and to our God, a day of rest. Today we have quiet and peace in this sweet little valley." His last comment of the day was, "Gave $50 to Mr. Hopkins to buy testaments and tracts for the soldiers." That sentence was the last diary entry until June 22.

While Jackson was marching back to the Shenandoah Valley, General Nathaniel Banks, with part of his army, retreated to an almost impregnable position just north of Strasburg. General Shields's division of Banks's command moved through Luray and marched north toward Front Royal. His orders were to proceed from Front Royal by rail to Fredericksburg to join General Irvin McDowell's corps as it marched south toward Richmond.

During all this maneuvering, General Richard Ewell was completely in the dark about Jackson's intentions. Writing to his cousin, Lizzie Ewell, the frustrated general lamented, "Jackson wants me to watch Banks. At Richmond, they want me elsewhere. When at the same time, I am compelled to remain until that enthusiastic fanatic [Jackson] comes to some conclusion." He continued, "The fact is there seems to be no head here at all, though there is room for one or two."

Ewell's reference to "elsewhere" in his letter was a directive from General Joseph E. Johnston for him to move his division to Richmond. But if Ewell left the Valley, it would completely undo Jackson's plans. Meeting with Jackson on May 18 just south of Harrisonburg, Ewell was determined to stay in the Valley unless he received a direct order from Johnston to come to Richmond. That order seemed to arrive on May 20. Jackson, however, convinced Ewell to wait until he could appeal to Lee for intervention. As the two waited for a reply, the entire campaign hung in the balance.

The answer came later in the day when Johnston wired Ewell, "The whole question is, whether or not General Jackson & yourself are too late to attack Banks. If so the march eastward should be made. If not, then attack." Finally,

Jackson was clear to follow his earlier directive by Lee: "Whatever movement you make against Banks, do it speedily, and if successful, drive him towards the Potomac, and create the impression as far as possible that you design threatening that line." Now having the men he needed, Jackson headed north toward Banks and the Potomac River. Just as importantly for Jackson, as well as the Magills, the Grahams, the Conrads, the McGuires and hundreds of other families and friends, he was also headed toward Winchester.

Relief from Federal occupation may have become even more important for the McGuires, since they were the victims of arson by the Union occupiers at about the time Jackson was moving north from Franklin. On May 18, Mrs. Lee entered in her diary, "We were startled by the sound of the fire bell; a bright light in the direction of the Fair Grounds. In less than an hour, there was another alarm & opening the door, the flames were ascending somewhat in the direction of Selma [the home of Senator James Mason], but it proved to be the Medical College."

Winchester native and grandson of one of Daniel Morgan's Virginia Riflemen during the American Revolution, G.W. Kurtz was a member and eventually captain of the Continental Morgan Guard, Company K, Fifth Virginia Infantry. *Courtesy of BR/GQ.*

By order of General Banks, Dr. Hugh McGuire's Medical College, the first of its kind in Virginia, was burned to the ground. Mrs. Lee believed that "both fires, were for the purpose of destroying superfluous Government stores & preparatory to an evacuation." Later, however, she learned the real reason; "the burning of the college is [because] a skeleton of Oliver Brown [John's son] was there." McGuire's students, after the John Brown Raid in 1859, had brought back several of the dead raiders and used them as cadavers at the college. Banks, a Massachusetts politician before the war and an abolitionist, found the use of John Brown's raiders as cadavers an abomination and ordered the college destroyed. The remains of the raiders were buried to the rear of the college.

As Jackson approached New Market, he sent Ashby, with a large cavalry force, toward Strasburg to convince Banks that his army was headed north on the Valley Turnpike. Ashby, however, was to return just as quickly and follow Jackson, who was marching his command east through New Market Gap for a rendezvous with Ewell in the Luray Valley. With only a small force holding Front Royal, Jackson planned to march north, brush aside the small Union force at Front Royal and then pounce on Banks's flank and rear at Middletown.

On May 23, Jackson smashed into the small Union force under Colonel John R. Kenly guarding Front Royal. Despite a heroic stand by the 1,500 Union soldiers there, Jackson had cleared the town and captured most of the Union force by sundown. Receiving word on May 24 that his flank had been turned and he was about to be cut off, Banks began a hasty retreat north on the Valley Pike toward Winchester. Late in the day, Jackson's advance slammed into the Union force near Middletown while it was strung out for miles along the Valley Pike, turning Banks's orderly retreat into a rout.

With Banks's army disorganized and in full retreat, the door was now open for a return to Winchester, and the people in town were in a state of frenzied expectation. Kate McVicar wrote years later, "But April passed and the early part of May, with many rumors that Jackson was coming, until the people became worked up to fever heat; and when it became known that the outposts of Banks army were falling back on Winchester the people went wild with excitement."

Jackson and his army were equally excited but were also near the point of complete exhaustion. After marching over 120 miles in less than a week, they were within fifteen miles of Winchester with Banks's army on the run. Fighting for almost every inch of ground from Middletown through Newtown (Stephens City), the Valley Pike was lit up with burning supply wagons as Banks's army hastily retreated. "The last stand of the rear guard was close to Stephens City and all the guns of our battery were engaged," Robert Barton remembered. "We lost a man or two and some horses, but we pushed the enemy back and drove them hurriedly through the town. By this time it was near 10 o'clock [in the evening]."

To the cheers of the locals, Barton, along with his brothers, had the unique experience of fighting on the ground of their own family home, Springdale:

> *Those in front had gotten down to the bridge that crosses the Opequon. We halted in the road, while the second regiment in our rear, led by my brother* [Strother], *who was an officer in Company F, and knew well the lay of the land, quickly climbed a stone fence and moved rapidly along through the* [Springdale] *barnyard and thence to the rear of the house.*

Despite the urgency of the moment, Robert Barton could not resist the urge to take advantage of the situation. Passing by the front door of his family home, "As we went by the Springdale gate…I tried to open it, that I might get a glass of milk or water, which I needed very much." Unable to open the gate, he noticed why; "looking down I discovered a dead Federal soldier with a bullet through his head, and his head against the gate." After viewing the gruesome site, "I made no further effort to get in but hurried on to join my slowly moving company."

G.W. Kurtz also had a memorable experience on the road to Winchester that night, and this one was with Stonewall Jackson. Kurtz remembered, "We pushed them all night of the 24th. Genl. Jackson sent for me. I found

Colonel John Henry Stover Funk, a Winchester native and doctor who rose from company commander of the Marion Rifles, Company A, Fifth Virginia Infantry, to command of the Fifth Virginia during the 1862 Shenandoah Valley Campaign. *Courtesy of BR/GQ.*

him at Bartonsville [Robert Barton's home]." After reporting to Jackson, he ordered Kurtz, "Take Company A with your own Company and push on towards Winchester." Kurtz continued, "Every time we fired upon the Pickets, I reported to Jackson." The general was easy to find since he was riding right behind Kurtz.

Fighting all the way, the Winchester captain kept up the advance for about a mile to Kernstown. He stopped at a house where he found, in the stable, "two cavalry horses with saddles and bridles. I led them by the bridle to the Pike and gave them to Col. Baylor and Col. [John Henry] Funk." Jackson later complimented Kurtz, saying that his small command had "accomplished more than if we had gone into six Battles."

It was at this point that exhaustion overtook Jackson's entire force and did what two Union armies could not do. The Valley Pike was blocked by the wreckage of Banks's army, and it was difficult to make much progress. Almost all of the men in Jackson's command had been marching and fighting for over twenty-four hours and had not eaten since the fighting began at Front Royal. To make matters worse, many of Ashby's cavalrymen were pillaging the deserted supply wagons. Jackson, who was now less than ten miles from downtown Winchester, rode with the advance and pushed his men almost to the point of cruelty.

After his defeat at Kernstown, he knew the importance of taking the hills south of town, which had been his downfall two months earlier. When Colonel Samuel Fulkerson, who commanded one of Jackson's brigades, approached him, he told Jackson, "My men are falling by the roadside. Unless they are rested, I shall be able to present but a thin line tomorrow." Jackson had great respect for Fulkerson but still insisted, "The line of hills southwest of Winchester must be occupied by the enemy's artillery. My own must be there and in position by daylight. You shall, however, have two hours rest."

With that order, everyone in the column fell by the roadside and was immediately sound asleep. Everyone, that is, except Jackson, who continued to view reports and instruct skirmishers. As Jackson aroused his men at 4:00 a. m. on May 25, he had Banks exactly where he wanted him. With the twin defeats at Front Royal and Middletown, Banks's scattered army could only muster about two brigades for the defense of Winchester. Jackson, in spite of the exhaustion of his men, had three times that number. It was also the Sabbath, and Jackson, for the third time in his career as Confederate soldier, ignored it and attacked. It would also be a day that the people of Winchester would never forget.

While Jackson approached Winchester from the south, Ewell's division was moving toward the Valley town from the southeast along the Front

Robert Barton of the Rockbridge Artillery. This picture was taken in the 1890s while Barton was serving as mayor of Winchester, Virginia. *Courtesy of WFCHS.*

Royal Road. Banks sent about one thousand men to contend with Ewell and put the majority of his command in a strong defensive position across the Valley Pike on Bowers Hill just south of town. The Stonewall Brigade, which was in the advance, attacked Banks's position immediately upon arriving at the battlefield. When the assault stalled, Jackson ordered up three batteries, and an hour-long battle between Jackson's guns and the Federal artillery still resulted in a stalemate.

As reinforcements were thrown into the action, it became obvious that the strong Union line in front of Jackson was not going to budge. With Union forces slowly moving around Jackson's left flank, he called on General Richard Taylor's Louisiana brigade to dislodge them. Taylor, the son of President Zachery Taylor and the brother of Winchester resident Betty Taylor Dandridge, decided to flank the Union position on Bowers Hill. Moving to his left, Taylor positioned his men beyond the western flank of the Union forces defending Bowers Hill and attacked. The charge of his Louisiana brigade, along with pressure from Ewell's division to the right of the Union line, completely collapsed all resistance, and Banks's men fled north in wild confusion through the streets of Winchester.

Winchester, Virginia, can rightfully claim to have one of the richest histories of any city or town in the United States. Here, George Washington lived and worked, learned the soldier's craft that would play an indispensible role in the founding of the United States and was elected to his first political office. In the streets of Winchester, General Daniel Morgan's Virginia Riflemen, the most celebrated regiment in the American Revolution, was mustered into service. The town has been the home of senators, governors and even a famous explorer, but there was never, in the more than 250-year history of the Valley town, a day like May 25, 1862.

As Banks's badly defeated army poured north through the streets of Winchester, the townspeople, with the battle still raging, came rushing out of their homes in wild celebration. It was reported by several Union soldiers that not only did they celebrate, but also many retrieved weapons from their homes and fired on the retreating Union soldiers. Kate McVicar remembered:

> *Now the Stars and Bars were in sight and the wildest enthusiasm prevailed. Heeding not the stray shots, old and young, rushed out to greet them…and husbands, brothers, sons, and sweet hearts rushed from the ranks for a momentary greeting to their home and loved ones. But why try to describe the indescribable! Those who took part in it can recall it all; those who did not could not, would not believe in all that happened on that day of days, the likes of which had never been seen before.*

Mrs. Lee, who was so overcome by the event that it took two days for her to calm herself, wrote about that eventful Sunday: "In the midst of them; one [Union] officer called out, 'ladies, they were too much for us' & I said I was glad to hear it & told him goodbye. I had expected that they would fire on us, if they were ever driven out of Winchester, but I forgot everything, but the joy of our deliverance." Later in her diary, she wrote, "Then we all rushed out & the streets resounded with our shouts & cheers as soldier after soldier, our own men came rushing by; we shook hands with all who would stop long enough."

It was not just the women who were wild with passion. Robert Barton, in his memoirs, recalled, "I hurried on to Winchester, reaching there to be in the melee of the fighting through the streets; to see the women rush out heedless of the shots and embrace their brothers and friends and all the people wild with enthusiasm and almost crazy with excitement."

Into the scene, riding down Loudoun Street on Little Sorrell, was Jackson. Upon seeing the general, the town erupted in wild celebration. His ride up Loudoun Street could only be described as Winchester's version of a Roman triumph. Jackson greeted the people warmly, but he still had much work to do. For the townspeople, the crisis was now over, and the time for celebration had begun. For Jackson, though, there was still a badly beaten Union army to bag, and he rode quickly north of town to supervise the pursuit.

Springdale, home of the Barton family, where the Barton brothers fought in their front yard during the opening phases of the First Battle of Winchester, May 25, 1852. *Courtesy of WDCHS.*

Unfortunately, Ashby's cavalry, which had become disorganized during the pursuit from Middletown, was nowhere to be found. Jackson's infantrymen were able to capture a great many Union soldiers, but without the cavalry in hot pursuit, the complete fruits of victory that day were permanently lost. Disappointed and angry, Jackson was forced to abandon the pursuit. His infantry was exhausted and, rightfully, basking in the adoration of the townspeople.

While Jackson had pushed his men almost beyond the point of human endurance to win the victory, few in the ranks or in the town realized that their hero was also flesh and bones. McVicar, years later, remembered that memorable day: "We all rejoiced in his triumph as did the Israelites when Pharaoh and his great host of soldiers were overwhelmed in the Red Sea."

Another Confederate who was there that day remembered Jackson's part a little differently from the hero-worshiping women of Winchester. He recalled in the *Detroit Free Press* years later that "Gen. Jackson himself was so completely exhausted that as soon as he ceased his pursuit of the enemy he rode into Winchester, secured quarters at a hotel, refused all offers of food, threw himself across a bed with his clothes, boots, and even his spurs on, and was soon fast asleep."

10
"My Dear Own Father"

Jackson's victory was short-lived, and he held Winchester for less than a week. Pushing his army to Harpers Ferry, he was forced to make a hasty retreat when President Lincoln ordered General James Shields to move west toward Front Royal and General John C. Fremont to move east toward Strasburg. The attempt to trap Jackson, however, proved a failure, and he defeated both Union forces in early June at the twin Battles of Cross Keys and Port Republic.

The successful conclusion of the campaign was not without cost. During a small engagement just east of Harrisonburg, Turner Ashby, who had recently been promoted to brigadier general, was killed instantly while leading an infantry charge. His remains were taken to Port Republic and placed at the home of Frank Kemper. Jackson, visibly shaken by the loss of Ashby, viewed his body alone at the Kemper House. Not usually inclined to laudatory praise in his official reports, Jackson wrote about Ashby several months later, "As a partizan officer I never knew his superior. His daring was proverbial. His powers of endurance incredible. His tone of character heroic, and his sagacity almost intuitive in divining the purposes of the enemy."

The cavalryman's body was removed to Charlottesville for burial. His stature had already grown to legendary status in the Valley, and second only to Jackson himself, he was viewed as the greatest hero produced by the war in the minds of the people of the Shenandoah Valley. In Winchester, deaths among the young men of town left a great number of young ladies spinsters. Many, though, were able to justify their single status by telling anyone who would believe them that they were betrothed to Turner Ashby and intended to remain loyal to him even in death. If all of these Winchester women were

The Boyd house was used by Stonewall Jackson as a headquarters for one day in the fall of 1862. *Courtesy of BR/GQ.*

telling the truth, Ashby's legendary status should include more than just his ability as a cavalryman.

The people of Winchester were also beginning to understand that their town was vitally important to the Shenandoah Valley, and the events of 1862 were only the beginning of their sorrows. The town eventually changed hands over seventy times and was the scene of many bloody battles. The war also cost the life of many of the town's most beloved citizens. The three friends who had met at VMI and together commanded the Second Virginia Infantry would not survive the summer. Colonel James Allen and Major Frank Jones were both killed at the Battle of Gaines's Mill a month after their triumph in the streets of Winchester. Two months later, Colonel Lawson Botts, now in command of the Second Virginia, was killed at the Second Battle of Manassas.

Robert Barton survived the war but was discharged after he broke down during the Battle of Port Republic. His brother, Marshall Barton, who had written the poem calling Jackson "Hickory" and saw the stamp of "genius" in his VMI professor, breathed his last on May 25, 1862, dying within a mile of his family home. The battle at Winchester had also reduced the famous "Three Bobs" of the Rockbridge Artillery to two; Bob Mims was killed in the battle.

Stonewall Jackson only visited Winchester once after the end of his famous Valley Campaign. As commander of the Second Corps of General Robert E. Lee's Army of Northern Virginia, he camped near Winchester for six weeks after the Battle of Antietam in the fall of 1862. His duties, however, kept him at the Second Corps camp at Bunker Hill, just a few miles north of Winchester. His campaigns of 1862, which began with the Battle of McDowell and ended at Antietam, had reduced his command to just a shadow of what it had been a few months earlier.

The extended rest was desperately needed and allowed the wounded and those broken down to rejoin the army. After camping at Bunker Hill for a week, Jackson's strength rose from fewer than eleven thousand to nearly nineteen thousand men. Those men were also very different from the soldiers with him at Swift Run Gap five months earlier. These men had been toughened by bloody battles and hard marches into what many historians believe was the finest group of soldiers the United States has ever produced.

Among those tested veterans were many Winchester natives who had transformed themselves from farmers, clerks and shopkeepers into some of the best soldiers in the corps. G.W. Kurtz, who had joined the Continental Morgan Guards as a private in 1861, was now its company commander.

Colonel Frederick W. Holliday, a Winchester lawyer who rose from company commander of the Mountain Rangers, Thirty-third Virginia Infantry, to commander of the Thirty-third Virginia Infantry. Lost to the service after being wounded at the Battle of Cedar Mountain, Holliday was later elected governor of Virginia. *Courtesy of WFCHS.*

Captain John Henry Funk of the Marion Rifles settled into camp at Bunker Hill as colonel of the Fifth Virginia Infantry. Frederick Holliday, who had begun his service as company commander of the Mountain Rangers of the Thirty-third Virginia Infantry, was not with his company at Bunker Hill. He was lost to the service at the Battle of Cedar Mountain, where, as colonel, Holliday commanded the Thirty-third Virginia.

With the need to restore his corps and a large Union army hovering just across the Potomac River, Jackson had little time for socializing in Winchester. He did visit the Grahams as often as he could, but these visits were very short. He also found time to pen a few letters to his wife. On October 3, he wrote, "Our friend, Mrs. Graham, of Winchester, sent me two nice sponge-cakes last week, and a Mrs. Vilwig, of the same place, sent me an excellent arm-chair for camp use. I wish I could keep it until the close of the war, as I think my *esposa* would enjoy it."

By late October, he lamented to Mary Anna that, "although I greatly desire to see our much-prized Winchester friends, it has not been my privilege to visit the town since May." Jackson did mention that Dr. Hunter McGuire had managed to find a camp stove for him, "in consequence, to-day, I am comparatively quite comfortable." On November 20, he wrote to his wife,

The McGuire house at the northwest corner of Amherst and Braddock Streets was the boyhood home of Dr. Hunter McGuire and where Stonewall Jackson left to have his picture taken by Nathaniel Routzahn. *Courtesy of BR/GQ.*

"Don't you wish you were here in Winchester? Our headquarters is a large white house back of his [Graham], and is in full view of our winter quarters, where my *esposa* used to come up and talk with me."

Although Jackson was not able to spend as much time with the Grahams as he would have liked, Mary Anna kept a lively correspondence with Fanny Graham that continued for the rest of their lives. While Jackson camped north of town, Mary Anna, now nearing the end of her pregnancy, wrote to Fanny from Charlotte, North Carolina, "I cannot express to you the great pleasure & gratification your last kind, interesting letter gave me—my heart has been so much with my dear friends in Winchester & the desire to hear from you all during the dark reign of the Yankees."

After chatting about her life in North Carolina, the prospect of having a baby and the trial of separation from her husband, she concludes, "Give my warmest love to your dear Mother, & sister—I do hope it will be my pleasure to meet you all again—Remember me kindly to Mrs. Conrad & her daughters, Mrs. F.B. [Frank] Jones (oh! How sorry I was to hear of her husband's death) & Dr. and Mrs. McGuire's family. Write soon."

Jackson had one memorable experience while in Winchester during this time. While dining with the McGuires, Gettie, Dr. Hunter McGuire's sister, asked Jackson for a photograph. Agreeing, the pair went to town and found Nathaniel Routzahn. While posing, Routzahn discovered that one of the general's uniform buttons was missing. Jackson, who proved a poor seamstress, sewed it on crooked. The famed "crooked button" photograph became the most famous one ever done of the general and was his wife's favorite.

Despite Jackson's question in his November 20 letter, Mary Anna was in no condition to travel to Winchester. The general's wife, who had come to Winchester the year before on a campaign of her own, was in the process of successfully concluding that assignment. With a new military campaign in full swing, Jackson had left Winchester and was near Orange, Virginia, when he received a short note from Mary Anna's sister, Harriet Irvin, informing him that Mary Anna had given birth to a daughter on November 23 at her home in Charlotte, North Carolina.

A few days later, he received this playful letter, written in Mrs. Irvin's handwriting:

> *My dear own Father,*
> *As my mother's letter has been cut short by my arrival, I think it but justice that I should continue it. I know that you are rejoiced to hear of my coming and I hope that God has sent me to radiate your pathway through life. I*

am a very tiny little thing. I weigh only eight and a half pounds, and Aunt Harriet say I am the express image of my darling papa…My hair is dark and long, my eyes are blue, my nose straight just like papa's, and my complexion not all red like most young ladies of my age, but a beautiful blending of lily and the rose. My mother is very comfortable this morning. She is anxious to have my name decided upon, and hopes you will write and give me a name…I was born on Sunday just after the morning services at church.
Your dear little wee Daughter

Jackson named her Julia Laura Jackson, after his mother, and wrote to his wife:

Oh! How thankful I am to our kind Heavenly Father for having spared my precious wife and given us a little daughter! I cannot tell you how grateful I am, nor how much I wish I could be with you and see my two darlings.

Mary Anna Jackson with Julia Thomas Jackson, Stonewall Jackson's only surviving child. Sadly, Julia died of typhoid fever in 1889 at the age of twenty-six. *Courtesy of the Stonewall Jackson Foundation, Lexington, Virginia.*

But while this pleasure is denied me, I am thankful it is accorded to you to have a little pet, and I hope it may be a great deal of company and comfort to its mother. Give her many kisses from her father.

Three weeks after the birth of his daughter, Jackson and his corps held the right flank of the Army of Northern Virginia's line at the Battle of Fredericksburg. The battle was a complete disaster for the Union army, resulting in an eventual change in command. General Ambrose E. Burnside, who had replaced General George B. McClellan after the Battle of Antietam, was relieved of command of the Army of the Potomac by General Joseph Hooker on January 26, 1863. The defeat at Fredericksburg had reduced morale in the Union army to such an extent that it would be several months before it was ready to renew hostilities.

This gave Jackson a small window of opportunity to have his wife travel from North Carolina so that he could meet the newest member of their family. He wrote to Mary Anna on April 18, "I am beginning to look for my darling and my baby. I shouldn't be surprised to hear at any time that they are coming, and I tell you there would be one delighted man." Mary Anna had already left, arriving at Guiney Station, just south of Fredericksburg, at noon on April 20. She wrote later, "When he entered the coach to receive us, his rubber overcoat was dripping from the rain, but his face was all sunshine and gladness."

When Jackson descended the train with his wife and child, the soldiers at the station greeted them with loud cheers. Taking his family to the home of Thomas Yerby, "he speedily divested himself of his overcoat, and taking his baby in his arms, he caressed her with the tenderest affection, and held her long and lovingly." When reminded that little Julia looked like him, Jackson responded, "No, she is too pretty to look like me." On April 23, while her doting parents looked on, Reverend Tucker Lacy, chaplain of the Second Corps, baptized little Julia.

The reunion, however, was painfully short. After only nine days, Mary Anna and Julia boarded a train for home. Signs of an advance of the Union army were unmistakable, and Jackson's full attention was needed for the coming campaign. General Hooker's plan was to occupy the Confederate army in front of Fredericksburg while he took the majority of his army and marched west to turn the flank of the badly outnumbered Confederates. Due to difficulty in obtaining adequate supplies, General Lee had moved two of his divisions to Suffolk in the southeast part of Virginia.

Facing a much larger Union force, the resulting Battle of Chancellorsville was one of Lee and Jackson's greatest victories. In a desperate gamble, Lee

Photograph taken of Stonewall Jackson by Nathaniel Routzahn at the request of Gettie McGuire, the sister of Dr. Hunter McGuire. It was Mary Anna Jackson's favorite picture of the general. *Courtesy of WFCHS.*

divided his army, sending Jackson, with over half the army, around Hooker's right flank. Late on the afternoon of May 2, 1863, Jackson's corps ripped into the Union XI Corps, throwing it into wild confusion and pushing it into the remainder of the Union army near Chancellorsville. With the fight occurring in a tangled wilderness area where vision was greatly impaired, the shocked and bewildered Union army was thoroughly defeated. The stunning victory, however, came with a heavy price.

While scouting ahead of his corps late at night, Jackson was seriously wounded by his own men. Dr. Hunter McGuire arrived as quickly as he could and helped removed the wounded general to a safe place in the rear of the contending armies. When Jackson was sufficiently stabilized, McGuire examined the wounds. He extracted a bullet from Jackson's right hand, but the wounds to his left arm where so serious that it was necessary for McGuire to amputate it.

With the battle still raging only a few miles away, McGuire determined that his commander and friend needed to be moved to a safer place. The next day, a long, and at times painful, journey was made to Guiney Station, where Jackson had met his wife and child just two weeks before. There, he could be given better care and, if necessary, moved to Richmond by train. Mary Anna, who had not yet reached Charlotte, was called to his side.

One hundred miles away in Winchester, Mrs. Lee wrote in her diary on May 8 that an acquaintance, Nat Meade, had arrived at her door with "glorious news that Hooker had been compelled to re-cross the

Rappahannock, repulsed everywhere & with an avowed loss of 10,000 men." Later in the diary, she added, "Genl. Lee's dispatch, saddened our rejoicing, for it says our General, the indomitable Stonewall, is severely wounded."

The wounding of Jackson hit the Valley town like a thunderbolt. Late on the evening of May 11, she recorded, "No news from the Rappahannock except various rumours as to the extent of Genl. Jackson's injury." A few blocks away, Kate Sperry noted on May 12 in her diary, "It's reported Genl. Jackson is wounded—some say has lost his left arm, but I hope that's incorrect."

The sad truth was that, while recovering from his wounds, Jackson had contracted pneumonia. Late on May 12, the worst news the people of Winchester could receive arrived. Mrs. Lee stated, "All remembrances of the events of the day are obliterated by the calamitous rumours of this evening; the Richmond papers contain the obituary of Genl. Jackson. I do not believe it even yet, though the bare idea has given me a more hopeless feeling than any other event in the war." The Richmond papers, however, were correct. Shortly after noon on May 11, 1862, with his wife and daughter, Dr. McGuire and many other close friends by his side, as well as a large contingent of soldiers standing silently outside, Stonewall Jackson died.

11
Winchester Remembers

The death of Stonewall Jackson sent shock waves through the Confederacy. His funeral and burial in Lexington were as close to a state funeral as the Confederacy could provide, and his status as the South's greatest hero only grew with time. Many believed the defeat of the Confederacy could be traced to the day of the great general's death. There were certainly very few Southern victories after May 11, 1863.

In Winchester, the news was even more depressing since Jackson was not only the town's greatest hero but also a personal friend to many in town. Since Winchester was occupied by Union forces under General Robert Milroy at the time of Jackson's death, it took a few weeks before the Grahams could contact his widow. Milroy proved to be the most oppressive of the Union occupiers, even attempting to starve the women and children of Winchester into submission. Any attempt to send letters out of town was severely punished. Fanny Graham's sister, Mary Tucker Magill, was unceremoniously thrown out of town by Milroy for attempting to send a letter, as were many others.

On June 13, 1863, General Richard Ewell, now in command of Jackson's Second Corps, crushed Milroy, capturing most of his command and liberating Winchester. In late June, Fanny Graham wrote her condolences to Mary Anna: "I cannot tell you my Precious Friend how I have longed for the privilege of writing to you & pouring out the deep sympathy & personal affliction which swells my heart & mingling my tears with our sore bereavement & yours."

She continued:

> *And now that the way is again opened I have seated myself once more to commune with you as in happier days…but you know my darling how we loved your noble Husband, how we idolized him, how we, of the valley, felt as if he was our peculiar property, our Deliverer, & you can see some idea of how every heart bleeds at his loss.*

Dr. Graham had very little time to write himself, since he was well known as Jackson's closest friend and the town was turning to him with its grieving heart.

Fanny apologized for her husband, saying, "He is anxious to write & tell you himself of his deep sympathy for you & of his own heavy sorrow at the loss of such a man & such a friend." She concluded by wishing "the God of all comfort dwell in your heart & bestow upon you richly all those consolations which He alone can impart is the prayer of your fondly devoted friend."

A month later, the Grahams received a reply:

> *My every dear friend,*
> *Your Kind, precious letter was indeed a treat to me—I was so glad to hear from you again, & then the outpourings of your heart for me & mine in these times of great sorrow and trial, touched me deeply—I felt how sincere they were & that you knew my precious husband as few on earth did—yes, you knew as few do ('tho the whole country loved & honored him & I believe deeply deplored his death) how much he was to me, how my very existence was bound up in him, how I leaned on him & felt so proud of my noble, brave Husband.*
>
> *Your devoted friend, M.A.J.*

The two would keep in touch throughout the war when the ebb and flow of battle allowed it, and after the war, Mary Anna and her daughter, Julia, would visit the Grahams and Winchester as often as they could.

Unfortunately, Ewell's liberation was brief, and the Confederate army evacuated Winchester after its defeat at the Battle of Gettysburg. For the next two years, Winchester was a battlefield for roaming bands of partisans, as well as armies. Those days only ended with Lee's surrender at Appomattox, giving the people the even greater task of rebuilding their shattered town.

Since nine major battles had been fought within or near Winchester, the most pressing task was creating a final resting place for all the Confederate soldiers who had died there. Many were buried in the backyards of people's

General Robert Milroy was the occupying Union officer in Winchester at the time of Stonewall Jackson's death and threw many residents out of town for wearing mourning pins for Jackson after his death in May 1863. *Courtesy of BR/GQ.*

homes or in unmarked graves throughout the county. The town went immediately to work arranging the burials of these soldiers, many of whom had traveled a long way from home to lose their lives in and around the Valley town. Beginning immediately after the fighting stopped, money was raised, land at the local cemetery was acquired and burial crews were assembled.

A little over a year later, everything was ready. In memory of General Turner Ashby, whose body was reburied at the new cemetery, a dedication was scheduled for June 6, 1866, exactly four years after his death. When deciding on a name for the cemetery, the town had very strong feelings about using the name Stonewall Jackson. Most believed that name belonged exclusively to his hometown of Lexington, Virginia, and it was inappropriate to use it in Winchester.

They did not feel quite so firmly about using something reasonably close. They decided on Stonewall Cemetery, and as one local historian pointed out, "You'll notice that the name has nothing to do with landscaping. There is no stone wall anywhere near the cemetery." Winchester named it after the brigade Jackson commanded. Even Jackson insisted that the name Stonewall belonged to the brigade, not him.

On June 6, 1866, the funeral of Turner Ashby and the dedication of the Stonewall Cemetery drew the largest crowd in the history of Winchester. Veterans of Jackson's old brigade provided a band, young ladies who had lost relatives led the procession to the cemetery carrying wreaths and local

A row of graves at the front of the Stonewall Cemetery in Winchester, Virginia. General Turner Ashby's grave is on the right, with a large Confederate flag in front of it. Major Frank Jones's grave is three stones to the left of Ashby's grave and just to the left of the grave marked Thomson. *Courtesy of WFCHS.*

dignitaries spoke glowingly at the ceremony. Since the Confederate flag was banned at the time, flowers were placed on all of the 1,747 marked graves. The centerpiece of the cemetery, though, was a large mound containing the remains of 829 unknown soldiers who had died in the bloody battles fought around Winchester. June 6 was designated as Confederate Memorial Day in Winchester, and every year since 1866, hundreds of local citizens gather at the cemetery to honor those buried there.

Jackson's widow, Mary Anna, lived the rest of her life in North Carolina, raising her daughter. After changing her name to honor her father from Julia Laura Jackson to Julia Thomas Jackson in the mid-1870s, she married William Edmond Christian in Richmond, Virginia, on June 2, 1885. The couple had two children, Julia Jackson Christian and Thomas Jackson Christian. Sadly, two years after giving birth to Thomas, Julia, Jackson's only surviving daughter, died of typhoid fever on August 30, 1889. Her mother died on March 24, 1915.

As the years have passed by, the memory of Stonewall Jackson has not faded in the Valley town, and it is rare that a year passes by when someone or some organization does not remember Winchester's most renowned hero. Well into the twentieth century, local newspapers like the *Winchester Times* and the *Winchester Evening Star* featured articles about Jackson. One interesting twist that was popular for sixty years after the general's death was an occasional tiny feature entitled "Stonewall Jackson's Way." Based on the poem of the same name, it was a Confederate version of "Dear Abby" using Jackson's own words as advice on popular problems and issues of the day.

The most prolific writer on Jackson, though, was Kate McVicar, who wrote for both papers under the pen name "Nemo." McVicar published not only her own memories of the general but also those of others in town, allowing citizens to tell their stories about their favorite general. Tales as simple as offering Jackson a piece of pie or cake were as common as stories of Jackson on the battlefield by his veterans. Whether these stories were true did not seem to matter. What mattered was that the people of Winchester believed them and loved telling them.

Katherine Creech, great-granddaughter of Stonewall Jackson, kissing Gene Barry, star of the popular television show *Bat Masterson*, during the festivities at the 1961 Shenandoah Apple Blossom Festival, Winchester, Virginia. *Courtesy of the Shenandoah Apple Blossom Festival.*

One such story that made the rounds during the late nineteenth century and that Winchester residents today find particularly hard to believe concerned Turner Ashby. Although the town was adamant about not using the name Stonewall Jackson, it had no problem naming both its United Confederate Veterans Camp and United Daughters of the Confederacy Chapter after the famed cavalryman. After all, with dozens of ladies of the town, now unmarried and in their forties and fifties, claiming to have been engaged to him, what better name could be used?

As Winchester entered the mid-twentieth century and all the veterans of the war, as well as the civilians who knew Jackson, passed away, the legacy of Jackson became the property of new generations of Winchester citizens. The local National Guard company, along with all the other companies in the Valley, marched away to fight in the First and Second World Wars in the 116th Infantry Regiment, which they proudly dubbed the "Stonewall Brigade." It was a title that the unit successfully honored at battlefields in Europe, including the Argonne Forest in World War I and Omaha Beach in World War II.

The area had also experienced a huge growth in the production of apples, and in the 1920s there began an annual event that still exists today. The annual Shenandoah Apple Blossom Festival is a three-day celebration that features parades, balls, carnivals and, of course, an Apple Blossom Queen. Each year, a worthy lady is selected for the honor. Beauty, charm and elegance are the primary characteristics used to select the winner, who is treated to the best Winchester has to offer during the weekend festivities.

In 1961, Katherine Creech of Winston-Salem, North Carolina, was selected as the queen for the Thirty-fourth Annual Shenandoah Apple Blossom Festival. The slender, hazel-eyed beauty was a nineteen-year-old freshman at Converse College in Spartanburg, South Carolina. She also just happened to be the great-granddaughter of Stonewall Jackson. "That was a big thrill to her," Cortlandt Freeman, Katherine's older sister, said. "Winchester really made a big fuss over her, and she had a great time, and it was something she remembered for the rest of her life."

It was also obvious that the DNA of the general coursed deeply inside her. Transferring to the University of North Carolina, she graduated with a degree in elementary education. Like her professor ancestor, she also loved to travel, and her first teaching job after graduation was in, of all places, Libya. "Of the four of us, she was the most adventurous," Freeman said. "She was always off on some adventure. After Libya, she taught for several

Nineteen-year-old Katherine Creech, the great-granddaughter of Stonewall Jackson, posing for her coronation as the 1961 Shenandoah Apple Blossom Festival Queen in Winchester, Virginia. *Courtesy of the Shenandoah Apple Blossom Festival.*

years in Europe before coming back to the United States. Then she moved to California and taught there for at least ten years. She was the quietest of the children growing up, but she was determined to live an interesting life."

Like her great-grandfather, Katherine had a deep affinity for the Hispanic people, and when a job opened up for a director of Spanish-speaking students in California, she applied. "She was not fluent in Spanish," Freeman said. "When she interviewed for the job, she had to confess that she didn't speak the language." Her great-grandfather's determination must have come through during that interview, however, because "they hired her anyway."

Tragically, Katherine died of breast cancer in 1994 at the age of fifty-two. But also like her great-grandfather, her legacy still lives on in her adopted home of California. "She did a great job and took a real interest in the children," Freeman said. "When she died, we established the Katherine Creech Scholarship Fund in her name for migrant children to help them go to college."

12

"To Preserve, Protect and Interpret"

One Winchester resident who had just moved to Weston, West Virginia, in 1883 was very angry. After watching helplessly as the birthplace of Stonewall Jackson was torn down to make room for development, he wrote a scathing letter to the *Winchester Times*, leaving no doubt what his feelings were about the destruction of Jackson's birthplace: "That was vandalism. In other countries the birthplace of heroes is held as a shrine. This is the curse of America, being too material."

Winchester, too, believes in materialism, and the town has been consistently prosperous throughout its history. It has never, however, sacrificed its love for the memory of Stonewall Jackson for profit, and with one tragic exception, all the places associated with Jackson are still standing today. The one exception is the Kent Street Presbyterian Church, which was torn down several years ago for the construction of the offices of the *Winchester Star*.

The homes of the McGuires, Magills, Moores and Grahams are still standing, either as private residences, offices or a museum. The battle to retain these sites has not always been easy, though. A few years ago, when an attempt to restore the old Taylor Hotel failed due to bankruptcy, the gutted building's roof collapsed, leaving an ugly eyesore in the middle of downtown. Instead of demolishing the building and replacing it with a modern structure, the Winchester City Council is working to restore the building, despite the enormous costs involved.

The home of the Grahams, today a private residence, is also the home of a devoted admirer of Jackson. The two Presbyterian churches in Winchester merged in 1900, but the Grahams were allowed to live at the manse until

The Pritchard-Grim House on the Kernstown Battlefield. The house is part of the property saved by the Kernstown Battlefield Association and is currently being restored. *Courtesy of THL.*

their deaths in the early twentieth century. The property eventually was purchased by Will Parlett in 1925. In 1935, Parlett sold the manse to his stepson, Sebert J. Smith. Upon his death in 1986, his daughter, Suzanne Vaughan, inherited the house. Vaughan is devoted to the house and helps perpetuate one of the lasting controversies surrounding Jackson's stay in Winchester. Vaughan insists that the Jacksons conceived their child Julia at the manse, while docents at the Lewis T. Moore House, now Jackson's Headquarters Museum, are equally convinced that the baby was conceived there. It is a mystery that will probably remain unsolved.

Others have stepped forward over the years and—at great monetary risk, in some cases—fought to preserve the memory of Jackson and his Valley army. Over the last twenty-five years, Winchester and Frederick County have experienced a growth spurt. Much of this is due to an ever-expanding national capital just an hour away, and in a post-9/11 world, many people want to raise their families as far as possible from what many call "the bull's-eye." The ensuing development in Frederick County has been overwhelming, and many of the most treasured local Civil War sites are now endangered.

Since the Kernstown battlefield is located almost completely within the borders of this growing area, it has been a prime candidate for shopping centers and housing developments. With the battlefield almost certainly doomed to extinction, about thirty local citizens stepped forward in 1996 to wage what seemed, at the time, a near-hopeless crusade to save the Kernstown battlefield.

"The city and the county governments approached us," current Kernstown Battlefield Association president Gary Crawford said. "They recognized that we were in danger of losing a valuable piece of history to housing development and commercial interests."

Meeting at a local school, Crawford and several others heard a presentation by the two governments on the state of local battlefields. It was recognized that the First and Second Battles of Winchester were already lost, but they felt Kernstown could still be saved. Although neither government wanted to get directly involved, they hoped that a group interested in history would take on the task.

Local businessman Larry Duncan, founding president of the Kernstown Battlefield Association, burning the $4 million mortgage for the battlefield property in front of the Frederick County Civil War–era courthouse. *Courtesy of BR/GQ.*

"A month after we heard the presentation, we decided to incorporate and try to save the Kernstown battlefield," Crawford said. "Our mission was to preserve, protect and interpret the battlefield. Early on, there was a lot of trepidation. Almost everyone thought that this would never happen." Their first move was to borrow the money to purchase the property, but that proved to be just the beginning of a long road filled with many obstacles.

The owner of the property died in 1988, leaving it in trust. When an agreement was made with the banks that held the trust to sell it for $2 million, family members balked. Feeling that the amount was too small, the case went into litigation and was not resolved until 2000, with the price tag rising to $4 million. "That began the real challenge," Crawford said. "That was a huge amount of money.'

Few in the group, however, realized that the turning point had been reached when local businessman Larry Duncan was elected the first association president. "Larry Duncan's role was indispensible," Crawford said. "He brought the necessary brain power to the project, and his conservative business approach was the key ingredient in our eventual success. Larry kept us focused on the most important goal: raise the money."

With a $4 million loan now secured from several banks, the group went to work. They looked for grant money, contacted every Civil War preservation group they could find and traveled far and wide, giving presentations to service organizations like the Lions Club, Rotary Club and the Elks. "We would get anywhere from twenty-five dollars to twenty-five thousand dollars. But we were grateful for all of it, and no matter what the size, we tried to use it wisely. After a while, we began to see the loan slowly but surely begin to be whittled down."

The group, while trying to pay off the bank, discovered another expensive problem. The property had been vacant for nearly twelve years, and the buildings there were dilapidated. To restore them would cost another million dollars, but supporters and volunteers by the hundreds stepped forward to help. The organization sold memberships to raise money, and before long, the thirty original members had grown to over four hundred.

One important hero of the project never gave a presentation, raised money or did any volunteer work, but without him, the project almost certainly would have failed. "A large part of our success must go to Stonewall Jackson," Crawford said. "His name is magic in this valley. The fact that we were working to preserve a battlefield associated with him made raising money and finding volunteers much easier. There were actually two battles fought here, but had we tried to save just the 1864 battlefield, we probably would have failed."

In August 2003, Larry Duncan and several other members of the Kernstown Battlefield Association assembled in front of the Old Courthouse in downtown Winchester to burn the mortgage agreement for the property. In less than three years, the money had been raised, and Kernstown Battlefield was now the property of the Kernstown Battlefield Association. It was a stunning achievement that few expected. Duncan continued as president until resigning in 2009 but stayed involved as treasurer. "He saw his role as the one to raise the money," Crawford said. "Once the battlefield was preserved and protected, he decided to let the rest of us stargazers do the interpreting." Before Duncan retired completely from any position within the organization in 2011 and left the interpreting to the "stargazers," he performed one last act of community service that saved another local tradition.

Handley High School boys' cross country coach and owner of Runner's Retreat Mark Stickley had a big problem. His high school sponsored the Judges Classic, a meet that was over three decades old and one of the few of its kind in the area. After having canceled the meet twice due to bad weather, the school, which was built in 1926, was going through a much-needed renovation. With the high school campus full of construction materials, it would be impossible to hold a meet there for at least a couple years. Four

Local cross-country runners Jim Thomson, Adam and Chris Arslan, Noah and Simon Vogler, Mark Dengler, Chase Anders, Jean Sergile and Braxton Terry participating in the Judges Classic Cross-Country Meet at the Kernstown Battlefield. *Courtesy of Mark Stickley.*

straight cancellations would almost certainly eliminate the meet permanently, as teams would look elsewhere for competition.

Stickley remembered that several years ago when, while running, he decided to venture off Valley Avenue and check out some vacant property near the busy road. "The first thing that I thought after entering the property was that it was a perfect place to hold a cross country meet." What Stickley had wandered onto was the Kernstown Battlefield.

"When I was faced with finding a new place to hold the Judges Classic or canceling it permanently, I remembered that day," Stickley said. "I called Larry Duncan, and he was very excited about holding the meet on the battlefield. He gave me a thorough tour of the property and let me have free reign to lay out a course. It was everything that I'd hoped it would be."

Stickley's need and the objectives of the Kernstown Battlefield Association were a happy match. "From the very beginning, we had an idea of how we were and were not going to use the battlefield," Crawford said. "We were opposed to having stone monuments on the property and refused to allow any reenactments to be held there. We also were not going allow soccer fields and baseball diamonds. It was sacred ground to us, and what we were looking for was something that would have a low impact on the property. A cross country meet was perfect."

With the new facilities and the larger area for parking, the Judges Classic is bigger now than it has ever been, and nearly forty teams compete, with several hundred spectators watching. For the Kernstown Battlefield Association, it is an opportunity to share its hard work with the community, and for the Handley Judges, it's an opportunity to mix a history lesson with their meet.

It's a special place to Stickley for more than just running. Two members of Stickley's family fought with Stonewall Jackson at Kernstown, and one, Emanuel Stickley, died there while fighting with the Stonewall Brigade. "I'm about the busiest person at the meet," Stickley said. "But it's impossible not to take a moment to ponder what happened here."

Preserving a battlefield is an important part of remembering Stonewall Jackson, but to the people of Winchester, he was much more than just a successful general. To them, he was also a person who lived here and became a much-loved part of the community. To preserve and protect the memory of Jackson as a person, only one site would do, and that site was located at 419 North Braddock Street, the home of Lieutenant Colonel Lewis T. Moore.

After the war, Colonel Moore married Mary Bragonier, and the couple raised six children at the house known as Alta Vista. Moore died of a heart attack while walking along Rouss Avenue in downtown Winchester

Mrs. Mabel Aikin, the last private resident of the Lewis T. Moore home, showing a painting of Stonewall Jackson at the First Battle of Winchester to fifth-graders at Quarles Elementary School in 1960. The students are (from left to right) Anne Nichols, Cheryl Groves, Anne Kerlin, Scott Pierce and Jo Ann Sartelle. *Courtesy of BR/GQ.*

in late December 1897. The house passed through several hands over the years, and the city was concerned that it would someday be forgotten and torn down or fall into disrepair. Several suggested that it become part of a Winchester Civil War National Park like those being built at Gettysburg and Chickamauga, but it was sold in 1937 to Mrs. Mabel Aikin.

The purchase of the house by Mrs. Aikin, who lived there for the rest of her life, was a fortunate one. She loved the house and what it represented and worked diligently to preserve the memory of Stonewall Jackson's stay there. Almost alone, she took on the daunting task of restoring the house while keeping its history intact. Her stunning success was reported by the *Winchester Evening Star* four years later with the accolades: "Mrs. Aikin's home is newly renovated under her artistic guidance with due regard for the preservation of every original feature, and possesses a wealth of historic interest and significance."

One of the most important things she did for the preservation of Jackson's Headquarters was done almost immediately after she purchased the property. Seeing that the wallpaper in the room Jackson used as an office had deteriorated badly, and knowing that the great general had loved it so much that he mentioned it in a letter to his wife, she saved several pieces before having the room repapered. Over the years, she also made the house available for visitors and school groups that wanted to view an important part of Winchester history. One local bank praised Aikin's efforts by calling her home the "No. 1 Tourist Attraction in Virginia."

Despite her dedicated work for the preservation and use of the old home, many were concerned that upon her death, it might again be forgotten and lost to history. In 1960, the Stonewall Jackson Memorial, Inc., and its president, Jay Johns of Charlottesville, Virginia, approached Mrs. Aikin and offered her $25,000 for the house, $20,000 of which was furnished by the Winchester City Council. It was also agreed that Mrs. Aikin could live there for the rest of her life. Johns intended to open the house as a museum at no charge to visitors. The site was to be operated by the Turner Ashby Chapter, United Daughters of the Confederacy. The transfer was made in early July 1960, just in time for the Civil War Centennial.

Mary Tyler Moore, popular television star and great-granddaughter of Lieutenant Colonel Lewis T. Moore. Ms. Moore donated the money to restore the wallpaper in the Moore house that Stonewall Jackson wrote about to his wife in the fall of 1861. *Courtesy of the Shenandoah Apple Blossom Festival.*

Johns went to work locating artifacts to display and, using Mrs. Aikin's samples, contacted a firm in New York to restore the famous wallpaper associated with the house. Johns's actions turned out to be a huge success, as artifacts associated with Jackson were obtained almost immediately for display at the house. In March 1961, the firm of Katzenbach and Warren, thanks to Mrs. Aikin's samples, installed the restored wallpaper in the room Jackson had used as an office.

By the end of 1961, local newspapers hailed the project

as an overwhelming success. The former home of Lieutenant Colonel Lewis T. Moore, according to the *Northern Virginia Daily*, entertained "thousands of visitors this year from all over the continental United States." In the next year, they were even more successful, as the new museum attracted over eight thousand visitors and now enjoyed the status of a must-see attraction in the Valley town.

Mrs. Aikin passed away in November, 1975 at the age of ninety-one. She lived her last years in a nursing home in nearby Stephens City. Her twenty-three years of work renovating and sharing Stonewall Jackson's Headquarters was not forgotten. Local historian Ben Ritter wrote of his first experience with Mrs. Aikin and Jackson's Headquarters. Growing up near an aunt who was related by marriage to the Moores, Ritter spent his youth listening to his aunt tell stories about the house, the Moores and Stonewall Jackson. After returning from the U.S. Air Force in 1959, he said, "one day I just decided to go up to Jackson's Headquarters and knock on the door." Mrs. Aikin answered the door and took the young Ritter on a tour of the house. On that day, Ritter recalled, "I began my love affair with Jackson's Headquarters."

In 1962, the *Northern Virginia Daily* remarked, "Although it was not publicized other than word of mouth, Mrs. Aikin opened the house to the public during her residency. Her hospitality was extended to all, and people came from distant points, including a number of foreign visitors, to tour the

The Lewis T. Moore home. This picture was taken in the late nineteenth century with a Civil War veteran standing in front. *Courtesy of WFCHS.*

house." Thanks to her untiring work, Mrs. Aikin is remembered, along with the Grahams, McGuires, Moores and Magills, as one of the most important Winchester citizens in preserving the memory and legacy of General Stonewall Jackson.

In 1982, the Winchester City Council offered to take over the deed for Stonewall Jackson's Headquarters. The Lee-Jackson Memorial Corporation agreed to the terms, which included a refunding of the $20,000 paid by the council in 1960. The city placed the Winchester–Frederick County Historical Society in charge of operating the museum.

Of the hundreds of thousands of visitors who have toured the headquarters, the most famous arrived at the home for the first time in 1992. Mary Tyler Moore, while visiting sites associated with her family history, toured the house with her husband. It was a special treat for the famous television star, since Lieutenant Colonel Lewis T. Moore just happened to be her great-grandfather. Agreeing to help restore the now-famous wallpaper in Jackson's office, she returned the next year, this time as the grand marshal for the Shenandoah Apple Blossom Festival, to view it.

Today, Stonewall Jackson's Headquarters is still operated by the Winchester–Frederick County Historical Society, which is opened to the

Stonewall Jackson's Headquarters. This picture is of the side entrance that is used today as an entrance for visitors. *Courtesy of BR/GQ.*

public from April through November each year. Docents at the museum are selected for their knowledge of Civil War history, the history of the house and, most of all, their undying love of Stonewall Jackson. In Winchester, Virginia, at least, they rarely have trouble finding qualified people.

Here, visitors can see and remember a day 150 years ago when the little Valley town suffered through its lowest moment. Here, they also learn how a professor from VMI led local boys in one of the most stunning military campaigns in American history for the express purpose of liberating Winchester. Many renowned historians would probably balk at that analysis, but do not try to convince the docents at Jackson's Headquarters that it is inaccurate—or, for that matter, anyone else in Winchester, Virginia.

Bibliography

Manuscripts

North Carolina Department of Archives and History
  D.H. Hill Papers
Ritter, Ben, Private Collection
Stewart Bell Jr. Archives, Handley Regional Library
  Allan Tischler Collection
  Ben Ritter Collection
  Bolling Barton Family Collection
  Francis Jones Family Collection
  Holmes Conrad Collection
  James R. Graham Family Collection
  Kate McVicar Collection
  Kate Sperry Diary and Papers
  Kent Street Presbyterian Church Collection
  Louisa Crawford Collection
  Margaretta Barton Colt Collection
  Mrs. Hugh Lee Collection
  Richard Duncan Collection
  Thomas J. "Stonewall" Jackson Collection
Tennessee State Library and Archives
  Polk, Brown and Richard S. Ewell Papers
Virginia Historical Society
  Holmes Conrad Papers

BOOKS OF PRIMARY SOURCES

Adams, Charles S., comp., ed. *Alexander Robinson Boteler: Wheel Horse of Whiggery, Stonewall's Courier*. Shepherdstown, WV: Charles A. Adams, 1998.

Allan, Elizabeth Preston. *The Life and Letters of Margaret Junkin Preston*. New York: Houghton Mifflin and Co., 1903.

Dabney, R.L. *Life and Campaigns of Lieut.-Gen. Thomas J. Jackson*. Harrisonburg, VA: Sprinkle Publications, 1977.

Hamlin, Percy G., ed. *The Making of a Soldier: Letters of General R.S. Ewell*. Richmond, VA: Whittel & Shepperson, 1935.

Jackson, Mary Anna. *Life and Letters of General Thomas J. Jackson*. Harrisonburg, VA: Sprinkle Publications, 1995.

McDonald, Archie P., ed. *Make Me a Map of the Valley: The Civil War Journal of Stonewall Jackson's Topographer*. Dallas, TX: Southern Methodist University Press, 1973.

Stanard, William Glover. *The McGuire Family in Virginia, with Notices of Its Irish Ancestry and Some Connected Virginia Families*. Richmond, VA: Old Dominion Press, 1926.

Strader, Eloise, ed. *The Civil War Journal of Mary Greenhow Lee*. Winchester, VA: Winchester–Frederick County Historical Society, 2010.

United States War Department. *War of the Rebellion: A Compilation of the Official Records of the Union and Confederate Armies*. 128 vols. Washington, D.C.: Government Printing Office, 1880–1901.

ARTICLES

Conrad, D.H. "History of the First Battle of Manassas and the Organization of the Stonewall Brigade." *Southern Historical Society Papers* 19 (n.d.): 82–92.

———. "History of the First Fight and the Organization of Stonewall Brigade, How It Was So Named." *Winchester Times*, January 14, 1891.

Graham, Dr. James R. "Some Reminiscences of Stonewall Jackson." *Winchester-Frederick County Historical Society Journal* 11 (1998–99): 77–103.

McGuire, Dr. Hunter. "General Thomas J. Jackson." *Southern Historical Society Papers* 19 (n.d.): 298–318.

Taliaferro, William B. "Personal Reminiscences of 'Stonewall Jackson,'" Submitted by Ludwell H. Johnson III. *Civil War Times Illustrated* (May/June 1955): 18–19, 60–65.

NEWSPAPERS

Detroit Free Press
Northern Virginia Daily
Philadelphia Inquirer
Winchester Evening Star
Winchester Republican
Winchester Times
Winchester Virginian

SECONDARY SOURCES

Books

Armstrong, Richard L. *7th Virginia Cavalry*. Lynchburg, VA: H.E. Howard Inc., 1992.

Bushong, Millard K. *General Turner Ashby and Stonewall Jackson's Valley Campaign*. Verona, VA: McClure Printing Company, Inc., 1980.

Colt, Margaretta Barton. *Defend the Valley: A Shenandoah Family in the Civil War*. New York: Oxford University Press, 1994.

Delauter, Roger U., Jr. *Winchester in the Civil War*. Lynchburg, VA: H.E. Howard, Inc., 1992.

Driver, Roland J. *The First and Second Rockbridge Artillery*. Lynchburg, VA: H.E. Howards, Inc., 1987.

Duncan, Richard R. *Beleaguered Winchester: A Virginia Community at War, 1861–1865*. Baton Rouge: Louisiana State University Press, 2007.

Ecelbarger, Gary L. *We Are In for It: The First Battle of Kernstown*. Shippensburg, PA: White Mane Publishing Co., 1997.

Frye, Dennis E. *2nd Virginia Infantry*. Lynchburg, VA: H.E. Howard, Inc., 1984.

Holsworth, Jerry W. *Civil War Winchester*. Charleston, SC: The History Press, 2011.

Krick, Robert K. *Lee's Colonels*. Dayton, OH: Morningside Bookshop Press, 1979.

Mallin, Robert, and Richard Radi. *Ashby Camp Revisited: A Chronicle of the Veterans of the Confederate Army Who Lived in the Lower Region of the Shenandoah Valley after the War*. Winchester, VA: self-published, 1995.

McDonald, Archie P., ed. *Make Me a Map of the Valley: The Civil War Journal of Stonewall Jackson's Topographer*. Dallas, TX: Southern Methodist University Press, 1973.

Quarles, Garland R. *Occupied Winchester, 1861—1865*, Winchester, VA: Winchester–Frederick County Historical Society, 1991.
———. *Some Worthy Lives*. Winchester, VA: Winchester–Frederick County Historical Society, 1988.
———. *The Story of One Hundred Old Homes in Winchester, Virginia*. Winchester, VA: Winchester–Frederick County Historical Society, 1993.
Reidenbaugh, Lowell. *33rd Virginia Infantry*. Lynchburg, VA: H.E. Howard Inc., 1987.
———. *27th Virginia Infantry*. Lynchburg, VA: H.E. Howard Inc., 1993.
Ritter, Ben. "A Favorite Portrait of 'Stonewall.'" *Civil War Times Illustrated* 17, no. 10 (February 1979): 36—39.
Robertson, James I. *4th Virginia Infantry*. Lynchburg, VA: H.E. Howard, Inc., 1982.
———. *The Stonewall Brigade*. Baton Rouge: Louisiana State University Press, 1963.
———. *Stonewall Jackson: The Man, the Soldier, the Legend*. New York: Macmillan Publishing, 1997.
Schildt, John W. *Hunter Holmes McGuire: Doctor in Gray*. Chewsville, MD, 1986.
———. *Jackson and Preachers*. Parsons, WV: McClain Printing Co., 1982.
———. *Stonewall Jackson: Day by Day*. Chewsville, MD: Antietam Publications, 1980.
Sedore, Timothy S. *An Illustrated Guide to Virginia's Confederate Monuments*. Carbondale, IL: Southern Illinois Press, 2001.
Wheeler, Richard. *We Knew Stonewall Jackson*. New York: Thomas Y. Crowell Co., 1977.

Magazine Articles

Ritter, Ben. "Sallie Conrad: Henry Kyd Douglas' Inspiration." *Winchester–Frederick County Historical Society Journal* 8 (1994–95): 48–51.
Wertz, Elizabeth. "Stonewall Jackson's Headquarters, Lexington and Winchester." *SPUR of Virginia* (Autumn 1971): 34–40.

Index

About the Author

Jerry W Holsworth, who is the 2012 Winchester–Frederick County Historian of the Year for his book *Civil War Winchester*, is an assistant archivist at the Stewart Bell Jr. Archives, Handley Regional Library, in Winchester, Virginia. He is also a docent at the George Washington Office Museum, which is run by the Winchester–Frederick County Historical Society, and a sportswriter for the *Winchester Star*. Jerry has led tours of the historical sites around Winchester and the Shenandoah Valley for various groups, including the Winchester–Frederick County Visitors Center. He is also the author of many magazine articles for various publications, including *Civil War Times*, *Blue and Gray* magazine, the *Washington Times*, *Cobblestone* magazine and *Potomac* magazine. A native of Dallas, Texas, he has resided in Winchester for over twenty-five years.

Author Jerry W. Holsworth kneeling in front of the grave of Major Frank Jones at the Stonewall Cemetery in Winchester, Virginia.